MW00325660

Laureates of Connecticut:
An Anthology of Contemporary Poetry

Poetically
Yours
Tarn.

Laureates of Connecticut:
An Anthology of Contemporary Poetry

Ginny Lowe Connors & Charles Margolis, Editors

Grayson Books

West Hartford, Connecticut

Copyright © 2017 by Ginny Lowe Connors and CCLP

All rights reserved. Requests for permission to reproduce work
presented herein must be addressed to the publisher.

ISBN: 978-0-9982588-0-5

Library of Congress Control Number: 2016921515

First Edition, 2017

Cover painting: "Slow Gold but Everlasting,"
acrylic on wood by Gray Jacobik

Book design: Rennie McQuilkin

printed in the USA

Grayson Books
West Hartford, Connecticut

TABLE OF CONTENTS

INTRODUCTION

The poet Galway Kinnell once said, "To me, poetry is somebody standing up, so to speak, and saying, with as little concealment as possible, what it is for him or her to be on earth at this moment."

In *Laureates of Connecticut: An Anthology of Contemporary Poetry*, Connecticut poets, chosen by representatives of the state or of their communities, share a little of their poetry and talk about the mysterious process of illuminating life through language. Poets laureate, current and emeritus, of the state of Connecticut and of many Connecticut communities have collaborated on this volume. They are being named at a gratifying rate, and we apologize for leaving out any who emerge after the publication of this anthology.

What is a poet laureate? In ancient Greece, a laurel wreath was awarded to poets and heroes. Apollo, the god of music, fine arts, healing, and poetry held the laurel to be sacred. There is a long tradition of government offices conferring the title of Poet Laureate on a person charged with composing poems for special events and sharing poetry with the public. Seven centuries ago the Italians crowned Albertino Mussato as their first Poet Laureate, and in England, Bernard André was appointed Poet Laureate by Henry VII. Over a dozen countries currently appoint a national Poet Laureate. What do they do? They try to help us connect to our deepest feelings, to make sense out of the apparently random events of life. They find words for what it is like to be human, in this time, in this place.

Juan Felipe Herrera is the current Poet Laureate of the United States. The first laureates in the United States were given the title "Consultant to Poetry to the Library of Congress." The position was established by poet Archibald MacLeish, Librarian of Congress from 1939-1944. In 1986 Congress voted to change the title to "Poet Laureate Consultant in Poetry." The national laureates are expected to oversee a series of poetry readings and lectures in the Library of Congress, and to promote poetry in general. In our country, laureates are not required to compose poems for government events, holidays, or the like.

In 1985 the state of Connecticut established the position of Connecticut Poet Laureate. There have been six poets laureate of Connecticut. James Merrill, who served from 1985-1995, was the first, followed by Leo Connellan, who served from 1996-2001. Marilyn Nelson served as Poet Laureate from 2001-2006 and John Hollander filled that role from 2007-2009. Dick Allen was Connecticut's fifth poet laureate, serving from 2010-2015. The current Poet Laureate of Connecticut is Rennie McQuilkin, who has also been the Poet Laureate of Simsbury for many years. "When I am writing or working for the cause of poetry, that is when I am most fully happy," he has said. "This is what I do, this is what makes me tick."

Connecticut is very fortunate to have not just a state poet laureate, but many other poets who serve as the poets laureate of their communities. West Hartford, Simsbury, and South Windsor are among the towns that have had laureates for many years. Recently, many more communities have appointed poets laureate. These individuals serve as public ambassadors for poetry, bringing it into the public realm so that more people can have opportunities to respond to it. The Connecticut Coalition of Poets Laureate is a group that has been instrumental in supporting the work of poets laureate throughout the state and in encouraging communities to appoint their own poetry ambassadors. They are also sponsoring this book, so that the general public can learn more about the poetry emissaries of Connecticut and can sample some of their poetry.

Our poets laureate have organized poetry readings in their communities, some involving nationally recognized poets such as Richard Blanco and Ocean Vuong, and others involving community members who have been invited to share and talk about poems that are meaningful to them. Connecticut laureates have put poetry on buses and sidewalks, and have organized ekphrastic events where art and poetry "speak" to each other. In another approach to melding art and poetry, one laureate initiated a project in which poets and artists collaborated to make poetry stands that are installed in public parks. Community participation was enthusiastic when a town laureate facilitated the publication of an anthology of poetry by local residents. Other laureates have curated poetry columns in newspapers and magazines, and hosted television shows featuring poetry on public television. They have placed poetry books in doctors' waiting rooms and opened poetry retreats for emerging poets. They have worked closely with students, with seniors, prison inmates, veterans, and with people in various community groups. Some have written poems for special events and shared them with the public. The list goes on and on. Brief descriptions of some of these projects are included in this volume.

Also included here are poems by each of the laureates, a little biographical information about each person, and some commentary on aspects of poetry. Past and present living poets laureate are included in this book; it is truly a collection that represents contemporary poetry in Connecticut and serves as a reminder of the vitality of poetry in the state.

The poets included here look at the world from different perspectives, and yet they share a common humanity. Over and over, in ways that never cease to fascinate, the particular reveals the universal in their poems. They remind us that in today's world of instant sound bites, poetry is needed more than ever. It encourages us to slow down, observe, reflect, and engage more deeply with the world.

– Ginny Lowe Connors

Laureates of Connecticut:

An Anthology of Contemporary Poetry

Joan Hofmann is Professor Emeritus at the University of Saint Joseph in West Hartford, Connecticut, where she has taught undergraduate and graduate courses in the School of Education for many years, with special interests in creative writing and students with disabilities. She directed the Academy for Young Writers with students from the Avon, Bloomfield, Canton, Hartford, Simsbury and West Hartford public schools for over fifteen years. Joan received Masters degrees in English from the University of New Hampshire and Trinity College in Hartford. Her poetry has been published in journals and anthologized in books. She serves on the executive boards of the Connecticut Poetry Society and the Connecticut Coalition of Poets Laureate, is a Board member of the Riverwood Poetry Series, and is the Poet Laureate of Canton, Connecticut (2015-2019). Antrim House Books published her collection of poetry, *Coming Back*, in 2014, and she is currently working on a new manuscript with Grayson Books emanating from her work at Breadloaf-Orion Environmental Writers' Conferences.

ACTIVITIES

A variety of programs and events have been held or are in process, including: hosting a Sunday Afternoon at the Library Reading by Connecticut Poets Laureate; working with local students on ekphrastic poems and on poetry recitations; writing for the *Canton Connection* and publishing poems in the newsletter of the Canton Land Conservation Trust; holding An Evening of Favorite Poems in Canton Town Hall in which participants read favorite poems to the audience; reading at various events; installing podium-boxes with writing materials on trails of the Canton Land Conservation Trust; and distributing books of poetry to medical, dental and veterinary office reception areas.

What were you doing when it happened?

for Allison Doyle

We were driving on the Interstate
Clogged in a traffic jam wondering
What could possibly be the problem.

Slowed to a crawl
Stopped
Glanced at fellow drivers

No need to change lanes
We're in the right one
We're making progress

We've studied the roadside
Littered landscape
Talked weather

Ate all the snacks
Wondered about a rest stop
Repressed the need

Reminded ourselves
Not late, not expected
Happy together, why worry

It's just another hour or two
Handed to the road
No need for hurry

But you? We found out later you
Were told about your granddaughter
Your thirteen-year-old

That afternoon she was swinging
In a hammock tied to a dead tree
That fell across her, took her.

I'm collecting friends' donations
For a tree for your garden,
A memoriam planting—
A futile attempt
To complete our incompletion.

Matrimony

Long ago I married the forest
and took the woods as my lover.
In our early years I explored
her outer self, moved her branches
lovingly, felt her velvet privates
tingle in thin air of dewy morning
as she dozed a bit, resisting coming
into the day as though in vow not
to surrender her dear domain.
These decades later, an older
couple by any definition, with
roles long-ago habituated—her
smells and sounds memorized—
we share common calendar of
afternoons satisfied by seasons,
I more in love with her inner self
and her spirit in me.

How does the natural world inspire your poetry?

Aristotle said, "In all things of nature there is something of the marvelous." I agree. Given a choice, I choose to walk on gravel or grass (well, water would be okay, too!) rather than sidewalks or asphalt. My family knows my favorite colors are green and blue. I'm a toucher and a walker. I like the feel and smell of plants, seed casings, feathers, and even dirt. If I can't be outside, I choose to be near a window for the breeze and sunlight. The sound of rain makes me swoon, the sight of water soothes and excites, the changes in climate and our preventative and restorative response to them dishearten me. How does it happen? Who knows? It's my organic core.

How do you go about finding the right words to express your thoughts?

Language and reading are honey for me. Growing up, I had the benefit of some strong educational experiences. Put that all together and *Voila*, there's good soil for writing. I love the broad landscape, the grand sweep of concepts. But I'm also a detail person. Poetry is about the integrity of some mighty small units. For example, commas take a seat in the front row of importance! Individual words matter, tremendously. Natalie Angier, non-fiction writer and science journalist at the New York Times says, "The beauty of the natural world lies in the details." Altogether, then, poetry and the natural world are a confetti party for me. Imagine: I get to mine gems, select sprouts, dig for roots, let seeds loose—in the name of writing poetry.

Rennie McQuilkin is Poet Laureate of Connecticut. He has
taught English and creative writing at secondary schools includ-
ing Phillips Academy (Andover), The Loomis-Chaffee School,
and Miss Porter's School. In 1992 he co-founded the Sunken
Garden Poetry Festival, which he directed for nine years at
Hill-Stead Museum in Farmington, Connecticut. His poetry has
appeared in *The Atlantic, Poetry, The American Scholar, The Southern
Review, The Yale Review, The Hudson Review,* and other publications.
The author of fourteen poetry collections, he has received a
number of awards, including fellowships from the National
Endowment for the Arts and the Connecticut Commission
on the Arts, the Connecticut Center for the Book's Lifetime
Achievement Award, and the Center's 2010 poetry award for
The Weathering: New and Selected Poems. His most recent books
are *Going On: New and Collected Poems* and *A Quorum of Saints.*

A new book, *North of Eden,* will appear in 2017. McQuilkin is currently the publisher of Antrim House Books. For over forty years, Rennie and his wife, the artist Sarah McQuilkin, have lived in Simsbury, where he is the local Poet Laureate.

ACTIVITIES

Some of the projects that particularly delight me as Poet Laureate are the monthly poetry column ("CT Poets Corner") I arrange for the *Hartford Courant* as a platform for some of the state's most outstanding poets; my ongoing poetry series on SCTV ("Speaking of Poetry"); and the delightful poetry workshop series I facilitate at the Simsbury Public Library, where I have also helped arrange some interesting readings, such as the 2016 Memorial Day reading featuring the last three Connecticut poets laureate. I am also glad to be a part of groups helping to "grow poetry" in the state: the advisory board for the Sunken Garden Poetry Festival, two subcommittees at the Connecticut Humanities Council, and the executive boards of Poetry at the Metro and the Connecticut Coalition of Poets Laureate. Poetry readings (both my own and the many I enjoy attending throughout the State) continue to be a constant delight, and I have enjoyed making a number of radio and television appearances. Finally, I continue to publish Connecticut and national authors as the editor/publisher of Antrim House Books, producing about twenty books per year.

Hands

Descending from the second story
I steady myself, hand sliding on the handrail,
then polishing the knob of the newel.

Time has worn away its beige, revealing
the rose of earlier days and hints of darker
shades below. For over two hundred years
and twelve wars, such a scoring by hands.

In the wash of history, time shrinks.
I remember placing my palm on the red ochre
print of a hand in a Utah cave, surprised
by the almost perfect fit.

At the newel, I fit my hand to the backs of
other hands that touched its round in passing:
hands of lovers ascending,
hands of mourners descending, slow hands
of the old, quick of the children rushing by.

And I feel the hands of those to come,
the sad and the joyful taking their turns,
their palms brushing the back of my hand
where it rests on the newel.

Mark's Auto Parts

In come the wrecks to Mark's
and out the gear knobs, gas tanks,
radiators, speakers, mufflers.
Bins of parts.

The crummiest clunker is worth
Mark's while. There's an alley
of front ends—Beetles, Buicks, Jags,
a '49 Nash,

an avenue of chassis,
a park of gutted bodies piled on
one another like lovers. Everything has
a future.

All of which is very gratifying, a sign
of what we'll amount to
in the after time.

The loosestrife will take this, frogs
that, the earth will value
our humus, the cardinal put us to use.
Dismantled, we'll go far.

Please comment on the way small, specific details can work to suggest a larger theme.

I do think that images and not words should be the heart of a poem, and it is detail that makes images come to life—not just visual detail, but details of sound, smell, taste, and touch. At the end of "Hands," when I refer to the feel of hands of future generations on my hand as it rests on the knob of a newel post, the phrase "their palms brushing the back of my hand" is perhaps preferable to something more generic such as "their hands on my hand." And in "Mark's Auto Parts," naming all those lovely auto parts lying in bins probably makes the scene more memorable. As Theseus says in *A Midsummer Night's Dream*, the poet should "[give] to airy nothing / a local habitation and a name." Details, details, details.

What is the state of poetry in our state of Connecticut?

Poetry is wonderfully alive in our area, judging by the size and enthusiasm of audiences at poetry readings; the abundance of new poetry collections; the multiplicity of poetry groups; the surge in the number of towns, cities, and organizations sponsoring local poets laureate; and the appearance of poems on display stands in public parks and along nature trails. Book clubs are actually beginning to allow poetry into their midst!

Dick Allen has had poems in most of the nation's premier jour-
nals including *Poetry, The New Yorker, Atlantic Monthly, Hudson Re-
view, New Republic, Tricycle, American Scholar, Ploughshares, Margie,*
and *New Criterion,* as well as in scores of national anthologies. He
has published nine poetry collections and won numerous awards
including a Pushcart Prize, the Robert Frost prize, fellowships
from the National Endowment for the Arts and Ingram Merrill
Poetry Foundation, and *The New Criterion Poetry Book Award* for
his collection, *This Shadowy Place,* published by St. Augustine's
Press in 2014. His poems have been included in six of *The Best
American Poetry* annual volumes. His collection, *Present Vanishing:
Poems* received the 2009 Connecticut Book Award for Poetry.
Allen's poems have been featured on *Poetry Daily* and Garrison
Keillor's *Writer's Almanac* and in Ted Kooser's *American Life in
Poetry,* as well as on the national website of *Tricycle,* where he's
been the guest poet writing on Zen Buddhism and poetry. Allen
was the Connecticut State Poet Laureate from 2010-2015. His
newest collection, *Zen Master Poems,* appeared from the noted
Buddhist publishing house, Wisdom, Inc., distributed by Simon

& Schuster in 2016. His poem "Solace" was set to music by the noted Pulitzer Prize-winning composer William Bolcom and sung by choirs to thousands.

ACTIVITIES

In some Asian countries, entire villages have defined their purpose as one of sustaining with food, drink, clothing and shelter a nearby hermit monk in his searches and prayers. When a state encourages poetry through the awarding of a state poet laureateship, it might be understood primarily to be supporting the writing of what may become important and meaningful and necessary poems. And so I hope during my laureateship that I've written some poems and books that may bring waffles and electric blankets and smooth sailings and maybe some ideas out of what Wallace Stevens called "The River of Rivers in Connecticut" to our state's residents.

Additionally, because I have a background in practical politics, I hope that by my unexpected serving on committees, task forces, and by my doing talks and readings at such as the Governor's Inaugurations and the 9/11 commemoration I've convinced some in state government that poets can be trusted, even useful. We are neither jesters nor fools. Shelley called us "the unacknowledged legislators of the world."

I hope, through carefully selected public readings and writings and talks during my tenure, that I may have maintained the dignity of poetry and the worth and love of poetry against the dangers of its being trivialized by the slipshod, the casual, the overly personal, and the too accommodatingly friendly. I'm most proud to have not ignored either blackbirds or Connecticut's wit.

Solace

Newtown, CT

There are the fields we'll walk across
In the snow lightly falling.
In the snow lightly falling,
There are the fields we'll walk across.

There are the houses we'll walk toward
In the snow lightly falling.
In the snow lightly falling,
There are the houses we'll walk toward.

There are the faces we once kissed
In the snow lightly falling.
In the snow lightly falling,
There are the faces we once kissed.

Incredible how we laughed and cried
In the snow lightly falling.
In the snow lightly falling,
Incredible how we laughed and cried.

Incredible how we'll meet again
In the snow lightly falling.
In the snow lightly falling,
Incredible how we'll meet again.

No small hand will go unheld
In the snow lightly falling
In the snow lightly falling,
No small hand will go unheld.

No voice once heard is ever lost
In the snow lightly falling.
In the snow lightly falling,
No voice once heard is ever lost.

December, 2012

A Cautionary

How do you get through this life
with its broken keyboards, its green awnings in the rain,
a battered tree top and a broken knife?
(the old man complained).
You walk a little. You stop. You hurt.
And then you go on.

Why was there nothing, and then something
and here became ocean and there became plain.
And what can we do about everything?
(the young girl asked, performing a curtsy).
You walk a little. You stop. You hurt.
And then you go on.

What if he or she dies? What if she or he dies?
If you can't trust even a Presbyterian
who will water the zinnias? Who will rack up the skies?
(questioned the woman wringing her hands).
You walk a little. You stop. You hurt.
And then you go on.

Do you know the way to San Jose? What tripped up Sisyphus?
Who took the noodles from my Ramen soup and when
were you going to tell me? Can I survive all this?
(said the madman, a gun to his head).
You walk a little. You stop. You hurt.
And then you go on.

Isn't this nonsense? Isn't advice
a joke in the ear, a clot on the brain?
One lie to another, just to be nice
(sneered the face in the crowd who once had my name).
You walk a little. You stop. You hurt.
And then you go on.

You've devoted much of your life to writing poetry. Why?

I'm very tempted to answer, *"Ooooo wah, oooooo wah, ooooo wah,*
oooooo wah, ooooo wah, oooooo wah, Why do fools fall in love?" because
it's both this intangible and true. But I should add that on a
schoolhouse porch one night long ago I realized the only way
I could come close to communicating whoever it is I was, how
I saw, heard, felt and understood the world would have to be
through the use of written words. I couldn't carry a tune or
dance a jig or paint much more than stick figures. And when I
tried to play a trumpet all I got was *"Blatttt!"* But poetry, with
its intensity of sounds and images, brought me near to the inex-
plicable and gave me a runner's high. I was besotted with trying
to express what our crossing from the 20th to the 21st century
has been like and why we ate Cheerios and drank red wine and
stared so far into space . . . and how we tried to follow the paths
toward Calm.

How did you find your way from the chaos and horror of the Newtown tragedy to the serenity that your poem "Solace" seems to express?

"Solace" found me. I'd recently written an essay for *The Hartford Courant* expressing skepticism about poems written too close to events that motivated them. Yet shortly after that Christmas, the phrase "in the snow lightly falling" came into my head and wouldn't go away.

I heard children's voices chant the poem.

Buddhists teach that pain and suffering are inevitable for all. The only way to get through this existence during this time on Earth is somehow to learn how to *not desire* the end of pain and suffering. We accept how they co-exist with grace. In the acceptance of grace and slowly falling snow serenity may come.

Toward the poem's closure, into the poem came my belief that "no voice once heard is ever lost" and my additional belief that since life is incredible, not to be believed, then it's likewise not incredible that there is life after death. The belief in life after death (such as my father didn't have) is one of humanity's main bulwarks against despair.

I say these things badly. It's poetry, with its tonal and visual nuances, that we need to evoke what logically cannot be. If you listen to William Bolcom's terribly moving composition embracing "Solace," this is how the children took my hands.

Marilyn Nelson is an emeritus professor of the University of Connecticut and author of several prize-winning books of poems for adults, young adults, and children. She was Poet Laureate of Connecticut from 2001 to 2006.

ACTIVITIES

As Connecticut Poet Laureate I funded a couple of prizes for young poets, organized a big reading in Hartford for poets from various places around the state, gave readings at schools and nonprofit organizations around the state, solicited donations from publishers and culled my own library to put poetry books, most of them anthologies, in waiting rooms in hospitals and doctors' offices throughout the state, and wrote and published four books about Connecticut history: *The Freedom Business, For-*

tune's Bones, Miss Crandall's School For Young Ladies And Little Misses of Color (a collaboration with Elizabeth Alexander), and *Pemba's Song* (a collaboration with Tonya Cherie Hegamin). I opened my home as a writers' colony called Soul Mountain Retreat, and offered free residencies to young poets belonging to under-represented ethnic groups. Some residencies went to young Connecticut poets.

Entitlement

Millions of flowers in summer.
Millions of fish in the sea.
Millions of stars in the heavens.

Thou shouldn'st have! All this, for ME?

To Be Perfectly Honest

The upper limit of my cruelty
is set only by my timidity.
If I were guaranteed impunity
I've no idea how cruel I might be.

"To Be Perfectly Honest" is a very honest and revealing poem. Did writing it make you feel at all vulnerable?

The poem says it's honest. I've never been pushed to the limits of my presumed virtue, so I don't know how I would behave if push came to shove. I don't remember now how this poem began, maybe with an idle thought about my/our potential for good and evil. But it's more an exercise in meter and rhyme than it is a deep revelation of my "real self." I was too busy struggling with the form as I wrote it to feel vulnerable. The finished product surprised me and pleased me in an almost impersonal aesthetic way, because it seemed true about most of us.

What do you think your greatest accomplishment as a poet has been?

My rendition of Euripides' great tragedy, "Hecuba," which is published in the Euripides I volume of the Penn Greek Drama Series, is an accomplishment that comes to mind. I've seen audiences weep through two staged productions of it.

Hugo DeSarro was born in Hartford, Connecticut in 1919, the tenth in a family of thirteen children. Hugo was thirteen when his first poem, "The Circus is in Town," was published. His collection of related short stories titled, *For The Mare,* was the first piece of creative writing Trinity College accepted as a Master's thesis. He has published poems, stories and essays in a wide variety of publications throughout the United States, Canada, Australia and Europe and has received numerous local and national honors for his writing. In 2015, he was appointed Poet Laureate of East Hampton, Connecticut, and in 2016 he published his first book of poetry entitled *Stone Steps.* Currently, Hugo writes a weekly column for the *Rivereast News Bulletin* and remains active in the local community, giving poetry readings at community events. He resides in East Hampton, Connecticut with Marietta, his wife of 70 years.

ACTIVITIES

As a long-standing resident of East Hampton, I've always volunteered my time encouraging the reading and writing of both prose and poetry, especially through the library, the senior center, and the school system. As Poet Laureate, I am now asked to write and recite poetry at civic and town sponsored events such as Hometown Heroes, National Senior Citizen Month, etc. As a matter of fact, if I am not reading a poem, you can usually find me playing the piano at many town functions.

Stone Steps

From the edge of a narrow
and desolate road, the steps go up
an incline into trees, a stone at a time.

Ascend the steps, push aside
the branches, and from the top stone
you will see a clearing and vestiges
of a house no longer there:
the sunken earth,
scattered chimney brick
and paths grassed over
to the outhouse and the well.

Linger a moment—listen and hear
in the stillness the ghostly voices
and domestic sounds of a household,
long silenced: the voices

of children at play, the barking
of a dog, the closing of a door.
And should you be tempted,
in compassion, to pity those
who lived in so desolate a home,
in isolation from the greater world,
it is well to remember that the accurate
measure of life is what it is when it is lived,
not what it becomes by comparison
to another place and another time.
Life was here beyond these steps;
it passed on. It is the way of living things
on this orb, and the only certainty we know.

Triolets 1, 2, 3

Pale dawn has gathered every star
then strikes a spark and lights the moon.
Behind night's door, time drops the bar.
Pale dawn has gathered every star,
but heaven's gate it leaves ajar,
and day pours forth a golden flume.
Pale dawn has gathered every star
then strikes a spark and lights the moon.

Daystar radiant in the sky
dries the tears of early morning.
Soft winds welcome with a sigh
daystar radiant in the sky.
Flowers, sleepy-eyed and shy,

curtsy to the new day dawning.
Daystar radiant in the sky
dries the tears of early morning.

Night slips on his dusky cloak,
shakes stars out from its shadowy fold
that blink and wink like elfin folk.
Night slips on his dusky cloak,
as mist alights—pale phantom smoke
that veils the moon lest she be bold.
Night slips on his dusky cloak,
shakes stars out from its shadowy fold.

What is a triolet and why did you choose this form for one of the poems?

A triolet is a short poem of eight lines with a set rhyming scheme of AB, aA, ab, AB. The first, fourth and seventh lines are identical, as are the second and final lines. It is French in origin, dating back to the 13th century. It is not a poetic form that I use often, but it lent itself to the subject matter of one of my poems, "Triolets 1,2,3," depicting morning, noon and night.

You're still writing poetry at age 97. How does poetry keep you young?

I've been writing poetry since I was in grammar school. Through my poetry, I can share my observations about human nature and the natural world. At 97, I continue to see and experience things that inspire me, confuse me and concern me. Writing poetry at this age keeps me mentally active and in constant pursuit of the truth.

Alexandrina Sergio is the author of two poetry collections, *My Daughter is Drummer in the Rock 'n Roll Band* and *That's How The Light Gets In* (Antrim House, 2009, 2013). Her work has received national and state awards, appeared in numerous journals and anthologies and been given multiple performances by a professional theater company. Sandy frequently performs her poetry, often accompanied by her husband, pianist David Sergio. Past reading venues include the Mystic Arts Center (with Stephen Dobyns), Windsor Art Center, Yale and Wesleyan Book Stores, Julia deBurgos Park, Cheney Hall, The Buttonwood Tree, Manchester Community College, Gateway Community College, and a jubilance of churches, bars and libraries.

ACTIVITIES

Part of what I've charged myself with doing as Town Poet Laureate is to seek out the poetry that exists in Glastonbury and help set it free to delight, fortify and connect us all. In pursuing that task, I have presented programs on differing days, times, and themes, in an attempt to attract diverse audiences. All programs, which have focused on performers who live in Glastonbury or have strong Glastonbury connections, have been free of charge and have featured poetry, music, and refreshments, with an open mike segment when appropriate. One program, drawing an audience of 120 and entitled "Words and Music For a New Day," featured internationally acclaimed poet Ocean Vuong (a GHS graduate), a video greeting from actor-author Chris Lemmon, GHS student poets and musicians, and books available for sale and signing. The Glastonbury Education Foundation supplied funding and hands-on assistance, with additional support and cooperation from the Town of Glastonbury, Glastonbury Public Schools, and local businesses (Barnes and Noble, Whole Foods).

Every Breath

Every breath you take has, at one time or another,
been associated with another living organism.
—Martin St. Maurice, PhD, Professor of Biological Sciences

Borne on my every inhalation,
through the choreography of time's particles,
is an immortal connection
with ancestors of courage,

speakers of truth,
allowing the possibility that
life is vertical,
death an irrelevance;
that while traces of
Stalin
and Pol Pot
prowl through time,
I breathe as well
Siddhartha
and Teilhard
who in molecular incarnation
may well be
among those Guardian Angels of whom some speak,
leading me in a single respiration
toward Omega.

Old Is Not A Four Letter Word

Old
is October on an
Appalachian Trail thru-hike,
Georgia long past,
Katahdin looming,
the in-between revelations, despairs,
pain, amazements
having transformed the pilgrim
into one who has breathed the sky,
divined that it takes this long,
that much black water,

to emerge whole from beneath
questions given first voice in youth
about reality and love,
unknowable until reality and love
leap out, attack,
demand naked combat,
turn the abstract concrete,
only then to relinquish secrets
profound with the power
to set us free.

What makes you turn toward poetry?

Just about everything! Poetry's raw material is everywhere, and
I tend to find it leaping out from unexpected places, insisting I
sculpt it into a form that can be shared. Poetry is an art. It is a
craft. It is a means of communicating on intellectual and emo-
tional/ visceral levels. I think one is entitled to answer to the
name of "Poet" if what he or she has written can touch another
in some meaningful way.

Here's what I can tell you about my poems.
I've written them, sent them out into the world,
hope they will not embarrass me in public
(clean handkerchief, minimal gravy stains),
that they will speak to strangers
and most of all, that the strangers will speak back.

I write about those things that arrest me,
cause me to mull or giggle or weep,
about scraps of old conversation
that have taken up residence in my brain,
about unfinished business,

mine and that of others.

I count on the poems to be emissaries.
I don't let one loose unless I'm pretty sure
it will make friends,
be welcomed with a grin or tear
or guffaw of recognition.

Thus I would not suggest parsing my work
in an attempt to discern an intended "meaning."
Rather, I hope readers, both kind and critical,
might ask of any of my poems,
So what have you done for me lately?

Gordy Whiteman was born in Guilford in 1929. He writes of its rivers, shorefront, the town green, and the spirit of the people. In his two books of poetry, *Whitfield Crossing* and *Home Town Guilford,* he speaks of growing up in Guilford in the 1930s and 1940s.

ACTIVITIES

I spent much of the summer communicating with Lisa Lappe at the Sunken Garden Poetry Festival, who invited the winners of The Guilford Poets Guild High School Poetry Contest to read at the Hill-Stead Museum. Much time was spent tracking the winners down and advising them on different aspects of their presentation that required preparation. The readings went off without a hitch and the students were thrilled.

Jacobs Beach

1940

Clams so abundant that Rube
will fill his basket within
the half-hour. This early Sunday
morning tide, brought down
by lunar power, is dead low.

From the dunes that form the brow
of the narrow strip of beach,
on across the flats to the sandbar's
goodly reach beside the channel's
undertow, all is still, the lull
of time and tide invaded only
by the pluck and sluck
of Rube's calm rake
working to and fro.

A hungry herring gull hovers,
chiding Rube, eyeing
the slim chance of a quahog
for the taking. Rube's view
is toward afternoon: a firemen's
clambake on the beach, this future
chowder that he's raking, roasted
corn, lobster, and friends to help
him prime a keg to slake
a thirst that's in the making.

Nineteen Reasons To Stay In The Here And Now

I have grandchildren on my mind
    Who bring me back and bind
        Me to those years that didn't last
            Shiny mirrors reflecting on my past
                Breathing life into all I've left behind

Like you, there are times when I define
    Certain days of my youth as flying blind
        Too much playing loose and playing fast
            I have grandchildren

The drift of years has brought me here consigned
    To slower steps and energies purloined
        There is a gulf between our ages which is vast
            Yet asked to choose I doubt that I would cast
            My lot to have time's clock rewind
            I have grandchildren

Do you enjoy using rhyme in your poetry?

Yes, I enjoy using both interior rhyme and end-line rhyme. Both of these approaches to rhyme are evident in the two poems which I have presented for the laureates' anthology.

You are the poet laureate of Guilford. How does this locale influence your work?

I have been blessed with the ability to remember much of my childhood. As a result, many of my poems are about Guilford, where I was born and raised. The poems talk about The Great Depression, war, the poor house, what used to be and what isn't anymore, and much more.

Julia Morris Paul serves on the boards of the Riverwood Poetry Series, the Connecticut Poetry Society, and Young @ Art. She is a founding member of the Connecticut Coalition of Poets Laureate. In addition to publication in numerous journals and anthologies, both national and international, several of her poems have been performed in stage productions. About Julia Paul's first book, *Shook*, published by Grayson Books, the poet Ted Deppe says, "Julia Paul is a poet of fierce compassion and lyric grace… There's no hint of nostalgia in these explorations of the kitchens and detox centers of family history, the homes and homeless camps of the heart. Instead, the exquisite memory narratives in this collection journey into the past and bring back poems that move and matter."

ACTIVITIES

Since being named Manchester's first poet laureate, I have served as its ambassador of poetry at readings throughout Connecticut. Of course, I want people to realize that listening to or reading poetry, contemporary poetry in particular, is not lethal and can, in fact, be quite enjoyable. Being involved in bringing President Obama's Inaugural Poet, Richard Blanco, to Manchester's historic Cheney Hall, along with a dozen town poets laureate, was a milestone in that direction. The Hall was standing room only, and the crowd could not have been more enthusiastic! In addition, I read at the ceremony for the traveling Vietnam Wall when it came to Manchester, at the swearing-in ceremony for elected town officials, and at Manchester's Fed Up! Rally to speak out about opioid addiction. I wrote poems specifically for each of those occasions.

Emptying the Attic

The past, with its yellowed newspaper
skin and dim bulb eyes, sits
on its haunches in my father's attic,
ignored while births and weddings
and my brother's death catch us in a riptide.
The strong arms of the ocean hold us
while the thin line horizon claws
at our backs like the past. We tread, said,
bled, wed, dead while the past sits
on its haunches in my father's attic.

Impassive as ashes, insulated and silent,
it eats Styrofoam popcorn from cardboard boxes,
the corners nibbled by mice who leave droppings

like breadcrumbs. I follow them through a forest
of ancient leather briefcases with gold embossed initials
from my father's middle years and designer
hat boxes, rectangular train cases
with mirrors in lids from my mother's dreams
of beaches away from as many children
as she has fingers.

The past, impassive as ashes, sits in the attic,
watches over us like a grandmother
who wants to scold but holds her tongue,
an envelope sealed by moisture
from that leak in the rafters. Dust motes
in the attic, exhaled by the past, what I
breathe in now, in my father's attic.

In a trunk full of mothballs, the WWII uniform,
army-issue blanket, love letters to my mother.
In a box riddled with nibbles, photos of the dead,
who, in these pictures, are younger than I am.
They're alive and smiling, focused on their futures,
pregnant with new moons, before their consignment
to the belly of the past that sits on its haunches
in my father's attic. A tap on my shoulder
like a relative's gesture, a kicking-can emptiness
when I pivot on my heels. My flashlight beam
bores holes into the empty dark.

Gratitude

For the bee.
For the wings
that lift its impossible weight.
For the quick and quiver of silver wings.

For silver
For the silken shiny
sound of the word. For the lost ring
glinting in the sun. The color of rain,
for silvered rivers scribbled on distant hills.

For distance
from the heat of the stars.
A distance that creates the pinprick startle
of stars in the weight of the night, before the lens
of the mind's eye pulls back to the reflection in the glass.

For glass
come from sand
come from rock. For the mystery
of a fragile vessel, able to hold more
than its own weight, the mangoes at ease in this bowl.

For the mango.
For the yellow sun
of its belly and the sugar-drunk bee
that pulls us with it into the tremble of gold petals.

How do you choose the specific sensory details to include in a poem?

I would like to say my muse chooses which sensory details to include. Truth is I have no magic, although I try to incorporate more than one of the senses to give a poem dimensionality. Ideally, the sensory details allow the reader or listener to experience the poem on a more visceral level. Visual details come most easily. Words can paint a pretty reliable picture. The challenge for me is to allow the reader to taste or smell the apple that has wormed its way into my poem, or to taste happiness, touch sorrow, hear doubt. Stretching the imagination takes effort. It's my favorite form of exercise!

Tell us about some of your favorite poets.

The late poet Wislawa Szymborska ranks high among my favorite poets. Szymborska won the Nobel Prize for Literature in 1996. There is no subject she has not tackled. Her poems can be whimsical and profound at the same time. She is a master of irony and understatement. She came of age in Poland in the dark years surrounding WWII. Not surprisingly, war and terrorism are among the topics she writes about, observed with both a wry and wise eye. Her poem, *The Terrorist, He Watches,* has, unfortunately, only gained in relevance since she wrote it in 1981. Her signature humor comes through much of her work, and is evidenced in the poem, *Poetry Reading.* Her poems are captivating, unique in perspective, and timeless.

Susan Allison is the first Poet Laureate of Middletown, Connecticut. Born in Derby, Connecticut and raised in Louisville, Kentucky, she returned to Connecticut, where she attended Wesleyan University, earning a BA in African Studies in 1985 after mountain climbing and traveling through East Africa. Shortly after graduation, she opened an outlet for old and rare books, Ibis Books & Gallery, on Rapallo Avenue in Middletown's North End. The shop was transformed in 1991 into NEAR, Inc./The Buttonwood Tree, an arts and cultural performance space. It moved to Main Street and continues to be a hub of artistic and cultural activity. She has read from her work in libraries and many other venues throughout Connecticut and New York. She recently opened for Richard Blanco, the 2012 Inaugural Poet. Susan's second book of poetry, *Down*

by the Riverside Ways, was published by Antrim House Books in 2009. Annie Dillard calls it "the work of a talented poet." Rennie McQuilkin, Connecticut's Poet Laureate, says that "Susan Allison has done for Middletown, Connecticut, what Williams did for Paterson, New Jersey: she has seen past its pedestrian surface to its mythical underpinnings. She has written a book whose passion, honesty, and visceral style make it an important contribution to the world of poetry." Susan lives in Middletown with her husband Stephan, and son John.

The Good Life

The thing about good living
is that it happens, despite
plotting and planning, it happens
contrary to all devices. It happens
when you are renting the only room
you can afford and you somehow
catch the way the light is coming through
the broken dirty windows.
The door is open
and the wind blows in like balm.
It's warm and you see the colors of the gray, faded
frame of the door against the rust-colored leaves
in the small patch of jungle down by the alley.
The good life
comes through your eyes
and your ears and your skin,
the way a wild animal comes at you
when it is just curious.

Broomstick

C'mon broomstick, let's fly.
Rise above these rooftops
and soar like Demon Angels
to the moon.
C'mon broomstick!
Dust your rickety self off
and we'll transform this lonely night
into the holy fury of love's survival.
And we'll sweep like nothing
has swept before,
sweep the pale stars
right off the evening's shoulder,
roll into midnight
swift as falcons fly,
draw the moon down into
our breasts and greet
the wind as we turn
miracles out of our own
darkness, unashamed.
C'mon broomstick honey,
trust me.

Can the arts, and poetry in particular, really revitalize a community? Please comment, using your experiences in Middletown as an example.

As soon as I opened the door to my bookstore, Ibis Books & Gallery, in 1989, poets began coming in. I held poetry readings every weekend and some were so crowded people sat out on the sidewalk. I still know many of those poets; they are still writing – poets from all over Connecticut and beyond.

I feel fortunate for my opportunities to hear and meet and play with other poets over the years. In 1997 the International Poetry Slam was held in Middletown, Connecticut. That single week enlivened the town tremendously and people talked about it for years. Poetry is alive in Middletown and has enlivened Main Street. I believe that poetry is in part responsible for the revival of Middletown's vibrant downtown scene.

Mick Theebs is a writer and painter from Milford, Connecticut. His writing focuses primarily on the fleeting nature of existence and all of the joy and unpleasantness that comes with it. More recently, his poetry has taken a critical look at modern American life, specifically the crushing grind of the average nine-to-five job and the isolating effect technology has on person-to-person interactions. Mick writes prose and satire as well as poetry.

CXL

In 140 characters or less,
describe what it feels like
to hold a newborn baby in your arms.

Turn the camera around and raise it high
to get a good angle as you take a selfie
with the wrinkled turnip-like subhuman.

Instagram the new life and reap a bounty
of likes and comments in a flurry
of hashtags like #blessed, #newborn, and #adulting.

In 140 characters or less,
describe the black bottomless pit of grief and guilt
and the fall of Eden.

Set up a Go-Fund-Me to cover funeral costs
and collect a second harvest of words of encouragement
and "good vibes" being sent your way.

Create a Facebook event for the memorial service and watch
as an army of blue thumbs pointing skyward accumulates
as the majority of attendees RSVP "Maybe."

In 140 characters or less,
wonder if you have a soul, or
if your very existence is as ephemeral as the wind
and that any bit of documentation is another piece of you
immortalized in a string of 1's and 0's
thumbing their noses at entropy.

Watch as the retweets and likes pile
at your feet like the spoils of Troy
and wonder what's going to happen
when your battery dies.

You are both a writer and a painter. What motivates you to create?

The motivation to create comes from somewhere else. I think the Greeks had it right by chalking inspiration up to the daughters of Zeus. All I can do is embrace it and try to materialize the ideas as they come. I think everyone has the potential to create beautiful art, but many of us have tuned out of that frequency because of work or family or the million other things that can get in the way.

As the newly appointed poet laureate of Milford, how do you plan to use your position to reach others in the community?

Right now I'm focusing on forming a writers' group called The Written Word that meets regularly in Milford. We've had a tremendous response so far, which is really encouraging. It seems there are a lot of writers in Milford looking for a place to hone their craft and talk shop. Hopefully, as time goes on, Milford will be known throughout the state for its writing community.

Michael "Chief" Peterson marries social consciousness with mellow poetic verses. Born and raised in New Britain, Connecticut, he declares himself a man dedicated to his family and focused on helping our youth. As well as being Poet Laureate of New Britain Connecticut, he is the playwright and one-man cast member of *I Wish Life Had Training Wheels*, which was selected as a festival favorite at the 2013 DC Black Theater Festival. He appeared on Seasons four and five of the TV One hit series *Lexus Verses and Flow*. He is a three-time Connecticut Spoken Word Grand Slam Champion (2013 - 2015). Peterson was featured at the 2012 Kallio Block Party in Helsinki, Finland, and performed at the 2012 Olympics in London. He performed with Brian McKnight, Musiq Soulchild, and Ginuwine during the *Love Heart and Soul Tour*. In addition, Chief Peterson has showcased his talents at many high schools, colleges, and other venues across the country. He not only speaks about social inequities and individual struggles, but acts to change the cycle. He is a performer who practices what he preaches. From the high school where he works to the stages where he performs, this poet-on-the-rise is all about turning his art into action and inspiring other people to do the same.

ACTIVITIES

I am currently starting an after-school creative writing club with several teachers at my school. In addition, I am working on a huge *Arts in the Park* festival for the summer of 2017.

Where I'm From

Where I'm from isn't as bad as people always make it seem
Where I'm from kids are finding better ways than breaking
The laws, smoking, and drinking,
They're now taking a pause, stopping and thinking,
Making better choices to prepare for their future
Where I'm from isn't as bad as people always make it seem
Where I'm from, more kids know how to curse
Than write cursive, they use words
Like *lookded, hurted* and *worstest*
She said *Mr Mr, he lookeded gooood but his girl was the worstest,*
It hurted my eyes looking at her
And where I'm from, most people laugh & no one corrects her,
They just choose to neglect her
But that's nothing new cuz so many men have done it
Her mother's ex-boyfriend (her father)
Her own ex-boyfriend (a father)

Her sister's soon to be ex-boyfriend,
A father of three and two on the way
And it's so sad to say that too many men in this world
Have abandoned little girls or little boys for that matter
What ever happened to Daddy's little girl
Cuz in this world, yes, even where I'm from
I've noticed a pattern with men leaving their young
So the saying fits perfect, Like father, Like son
Cuz the boys aren't taught any better
But they learned how to measure cuz they learned it in the hood
And it's all good cuz school is for the birds,
So they get high off that herb
And hope Ms. Clark grades with a curve
So they can pass and graduate,
But where I'm from they're always a tad too late
Where I'm from, if it ain't one thing it's another
My 13-year-old student got caught smoking weed with her brother
Come to find out she's pregnant and so is her mother
And what bothers is neither one knows who the father is
But around my way that's just the same story, just a different day
Where I'm from isn't as bad as people always make it seem
So I tell my students to listen closely while I school you,
Don't let my shirt and tie fool you
I'm from where you're from, I've done what you've done,
Seen what you've seen
I was once in between a rock and hard place, just like you, yeah,
My father left me too
I've seen my friends die, watched my mom cry and been too
Afraid to try, I've seen my grandmother slapped,
My uncle on crack, I've seen a mother beat up by her daughter
And some honest to God truth, my great-grandfather
Was murdered over a quarter
Yeah, I received help from the state and damn what you say
Those food stamps were great

Yes I've heated my house with the oven
And drank Kool-Aid from a jelly jar
And the city bus was once my car
I've faced my share of adversity and overcome it all
They can't stop me, I can't lose, cuz I choose not to
Need help? I got you, we'll make it to the top together
Then scream
They may take away our dollars but they can't steal our dreams
We're all in here, but things aren't as good as what appears
To be seen
And remember, where I'm from
Isn't as bad as people always make it seem

What does performance poetry bring to the audience?

The sincerity behind the words can be delivered precisely rather than making a reader create his own visual as he reads. It's engaging and entertaining while still encompassing the essence of poetry.

Do you use poetry to connect with students?

Absolutely, it has been an awesome way to make connections and for kids to use as an outlet. Poetry is not just what I do, it is who I am and my students all know that.

Has poetry changed you in any way?

Poetry has saved my life. It has been the most therapeutic practice for me. Without being able to express myself through the word, I would have found myself stuck in some very dark places.

Dr. James R. Scrimgeour, first Poet Laureate of New Milford, Connecticut, is Professor Emeritus at Western Connecticut State University. He has been a member of the New Milford Commission on the Arts for over 35 years and has been writing a poem per week since 1993. He has published nine books of poetry, over 220 poems in anthologies and periodicals, and has given over 250 public readings of his work, including one at an International Conference on Poetry and History in Stirling, Scotland. Dr. Scrimgeour has been nominated for several Pushcart Prizes, has participated in NEH poetry seminars at NYU and Princeton, has served as Editor of *Connecticut Review*, and is one of five poets featured on the CBS-Connecticut Poetry Blog. In addition, he has published a critical biography of Sean O'Casey and a number of articles on poetry and drama.

ACTIVITIES

Some of the activities I've been involved in as poet laureate of New Milford include a Poet Laureate introductory reading at the New Milford Public library, a reading at the Minor Memorial Library in Roxbury, Connecticut, and a reading at the "Thanks for the Giving" benefit for Loaves and Fishes Hospitality House in New Milford. My original poem was read as part of New Milford's Memorial Day service, and I have contributed poems to the mayor's Facebook page. During my tenure as poet laureate, a poetry book club was initiated for New Milford residents. Currently I am developing a creative writing workshop for local residents.

After the Five Star Dinner

after the salmon with ravioli
and ginger sauce, sipping our wine,
and watching large steamships
chug in and out of Stockholm harbor . . .
each of those vessels gliding past

Millet's "Man on the Rainbow" . . .
background laughter of people
at the next table, while directly
beneath us, a private boat, with
four people, dressed in formal attire,

stepping gingerly to the restaurant deck . . .
beyond them—lies the bare rock,
that less than two hours ago was

covered with sunbathers—when,
after our ice cream—we walked past . . .

well, here we are, you and me,
basking in now, in today on an island
in Sweden—thinking wow—it's been
six years since the angio and stents
in two major arteries (when my life

was hanging, literally hanging
by a thread)—thinking if I were
my father . . . thinking thanks
for today, for this poem, for you,
genuine thanks for every day, for each

additional poem, and for each and every
one of the extra 2,323 (and counting)
days I got to spend with you—
my lover, my wife, my friend.

The Image

of the twin silver transistor radios
shining in sunlight and resting on beds
of flaming planes remains with us;
we can't sleep—the image returns

again and again—whenever we close
our eyes we see the stick insect figures
falling, one by one by one—and
the pair, the man and woman who jumped,

holding hands, is too painful to bear . . .
We force our eyes open, but still we hear
the background noise coming through
all those tiny black window holes—

the roar of hijacked engines fading out
and in—getting louder and softer,
then louder again—the rolling thunder
of twin towers collapsing into rubble,

steel girders twisting into playdough
pretzels—voices through the ash
and static, like the woman, married
for one year, giving her presentation

one story above the flames—her
"I Love You!" on the answering machine
in California for her husband to hear—
just one of thousands saying goodbye,

so clear a signal cutting through the thick
billowing acrid smoke, the swirling fog
of hatred that some call consciousness.

How do you choose topics to write about?

I try not to choose topics, but rather I let them choose me! When I am out walking "en plein aire," as I often do, I try to remain open to things in the environment (like a discarded orange on the beach, a daisy lying on a bed of moss, or an unfinished statue in a meadow) that are calling to me to write about them. It is not until I can answer the question "Why was this object calling to me?" that I have the focus I need to complete the poem. When something in my personal or family life says this is a special moment of human experience, I stop and try to get it down. (The why, in these cases, is almost always obvious). And when something like the World Trade Center disaster says, "You have to write about me!" I listen. Note: after writing "The Image," I showed it to a poet friend of mine who said, "How can you write about that?" "How could you not write about it?" I answered.

Who are your favorite poets?

The English Romantic poets (especially Blake, Wordsworth, and Keats) have been important influences on me from graduate school to the present. They have helped instill in me a love of nature, an interest in the human imagination, and an appreciation of the value inherent in the lives of "common" men and women. Other poets who have contributed to my development as a poet include, but are not limited to: Elizabeth Bishop, Emily Dickinson, Rita Dove, Robert Frost, Langston Hughes, Mary Oliver, Wallace Stevens, Walt Whitman, William Carlos Williams, and William Butler Yeats.

Lisa Schwartz thinks she may be the only town poet laureate who is not a published poet (although her local newspaper frequently prints her occasional verse). Although she has written poetry all of her life, her desire to publish is often overpowered by her dread of rejection. She served for several years as poetry editor of *The Newtowner Magazine*, selecting the poetry of others in lieu of submitting her own. Ms. Schwartz writes poems for town occasions, shares her work with friends, finds encouragement in local writing groups, and reads a lot of poetry, hoping to understand that which cannot be explained.

ACTIVITIES

In my first year as Poet Laureate of Newtown, I promoted verse through both the written and the spoken word. To honor National Poetry Month in April, I asked our local newspaper, *The Newtown Bee*, to publish one poem a week of my choosing. I selected works by well-known authors as well as local writers. My hope is to eventually convince the publishers to introduce a "Poem-A-Month" column to run in poetic perpetuity.

My second, and more ambitious, project was called *Risk A Verse*. Local residents were asked to gather, recite a favorite poem, and explain its personal significance. We chose a cross-section of the community, including our school crossing guard, our first selectman, and many others. This event was a resounding success, with close to 100 people in attendance. *Risk A Verse* has officially been deemed an annual celebration of poetry in Newtown.

Déjà Vu

Science says
we derive from the stars,
cosmic dust from a spawned universe
on a sprawling celestial spin
toward a place (or is it a time?)
they call Infinity.

The question is, Did we come from Infinity
or are we headed there?

I say it's both.
I say we write our script in retrograde,
believing that destiny awaits us
when in truth, the past lies ahead.
This is déjà vu:
the wiretap of the past whispering to our hither
like a benevolent phantom
who's dropped in for a drink.

Science tells us the universe is relative.
I say we're strung out on theories.

You'd think by now we'd have learned a thing or two
about knowing too much
(being older and wiser dust such as we are), but no.
We can't reconcile the notion that some questions
are without answers,
some codes uncrackable.

We Hang On

It is taxing to write about serious things:
    Violence, evil, death.
    But this is the work of the poet, isn't it--
    To give voice to sorrows unthinkable?

I have always steered clear of darkness,
    Preferring trivial spins to the brutality of living.
    Yet there are moments when my conscience howls.

I am a coward
        Running from a savagery that stills my pen,
        From the unanswerable—
From the cries of shattered hearts
That cleave a ruthless silence.

Emerson once wrote,
        When it is darkest, men see stars.
        I will bank on this hope,
        Though the scale of our grief
        Belies any dream of solace.

Still, we hang on.

Everything we know is threaded by contrast;
        The barkfly and the blue whale,
        The nebula and the quark,
        Stone and sea and sky.

We, too, are coiled in contradiction,
        Helixes twisting in a tandem loop
        Of sublime and monstrous.
        Could we survive without our duality?
        Love each other despite the lure of malice that
        Churns our spiraled history?

We cannot answer.
        Still, we hang on.

What do you see as the role of contradiction in poetry?

Contradiction plays a significant role in poetry and indeed in life. Human beings are not just complicated, we are vexingly so; our inconsistencies are boundless and unpredictable. Even as we project our best selves into the world, there is that inscrutable *something* that belies our benevolence. We may be kind and tolerant, yet we all carry within us the capacity for cruelty and spite. Perhaps this is why our most public display—our political process—is so fraught. We are an untamed compilation of virtue and vice, each in different measures and with staggering variation. Yet it is this very duality that makes us human.

Gwendolyn Brooks once said, "Poetry is life distilled." I am fond of Brooks' notion that we can condense our humanity into verse, or that poetry can deliver us from the morass of our incongruity. There is comfort in such thinking, like waiting in darkness for the promise of light. We are compelled to use the language of contradiction so that we may examine our frailties alongside of our triumphs: there is no understanding of peace without war, no appreciation of love without hate, no gratitude for abundance without scarcity. We must evaluate these contrary notions with equal regard if we have any hope of discovering our true selves.

In my poem, *We Hang On,* I ponder the question of whether mankind could exist without this dual nature of good and evil. A world devoid of wrongdoing would offer little in the way of spiritual self-inquiry, for it is the dichotomy of the universe that enthralls us. Why are we both good and evil? Is there a place for both aspects of our humanity? I believe it is through poetry that we examine these contradictions and seek our grander purpose.

Laurel S. Peterson is a Professor of English at Norwalk Community College. Her poetry has been published in many small literary journals. She has two poetry chapbooks, *That's the Way the Music Sounds* (Finishing Line Press, 2009) and *Talking to the Mirror* (The Last Automat Press, 2010). She also co-edited a collection of essays on women's justice titled *(Re)Interpretations: The Shapes of Justice in Women's Experience* (2009). Her mystery novel, *Shadow Notes,* was released by Barking Rain Press in May 2016, and a full length collection of poetry, *"Do You Expect Your Art to Answer You?"* was released by Futurecycle Press in January of 2017. She is the Poet Laureate of Norwalk, Connecticut.

ACTIVITIES

My focus as laureate is to make poetry public. To that end, we started by putting poems in the Norwalk buses and we're currently putting poems on the sidewalk in South Norwalk (with special paint, so they only show up when it rains). I've worked with children, encouraging them to write poems about their identities, these poems then being presented at a town festival; and I'm bringing poets in to our public library for a series entitled "Poets in Conversation."

Tug

You
are a silken thread
knotted and sewn into my heart.
Every turn
      to look at a soaring eagle
      to smell the floating breeze
      to taste the first flake of snow
tugs the thread,
sends a tiny shiver of shock
to remind me
you're not here
and won't be ever.

Sewn into your heart
is the other end,
knotted just under the fragile
epicardium.
We both must move
so very gently.

The cord itself remains unfailing:
even if it is dirtied or worn by ice or heat,
ridden by sparrows and picked apart by crows,
its fibers never lose their integrity:
never fray or shred
or lessen in tension or
their ability to signal across
the great distance
of our unremitting singularity
to say
I'm here.
I'm waiting.

Woman

Street Scene: Exhausted Woman Seated on Stoop,
New York City, Leon Levinstein

She sat on steps
at the edge of the avenue,
half in the light of day,
half in the light of evening,
her shoulders bent like osteoporosis,
bones compacting into stone dust.
People keep handing me things, she said.
At first, a half-filled coffee cup,
a plate with a little leftover fruit.
Could you clean these? they ask.
Wash them and tuck them
where we can't see them anymore.

Then, the things got bigger.

They handed me their cheating husbands,
their children's empty beer cans and stolen goods,
their parents' beatings and curses,
their dead friends.

Me, she said, *I'm still carrying that coffee cup,*
looking for a place to put it down,
to put it all down.
Her arms and legs shone dark against the white-painted stairs.

Why do you want to put poetry on buses and sidewalks, and how do you think people will react to seeing poems in these unexpected places?

Putting poetry on buses and sidewalks is part of the mission of my laureateship. More than that, I like the idea of public art. Art on a bus or on a sidewalk is free. It doesn't require going anywhere special; instead, the art appears as part of one's daily routine. A person can literally trip over it. Perhaps, in seeing it day after day, it becomes part of us and we a part of it. I hope people will react with delight, will be inspired, will be comforted.

Why should a community appoint a poet laureate?

I would encourage every community to appoint a poet laureate because sometimes words get left out when communities promote the arts. The visual arts, music, even dance are seemingly more accessible art forms, but poetry has been telling our stories and recording our pains and desires for centuries, and many young people are drawn to its music and energy. Encouraging that adds to the richness of the artistic community. Also, appointing a poet laureate encourages awareness of and engagement with language. Poetry requires us to slow down, to reread, to think—things that, in our fast-paced lives, we often don't prioritize. A poet laureate can offer a community opportunities to think about deeper human concerns: love, death, pain.

Patricia Horn O'Brien is a graduate of Columbia School of Social Work and has worked and volunteered as a social worker throughout her adult life. She's a member of the *Guilford Poets Guild* and recently co-founded a local poetry group, *CT River Poets*. She's helped in the establishment of Prison Hospice in three Connecticut prisons and facilitated poetry workshops at York Correctional Institution. She initiated the ongoing program, *Paintings and Poetry*, at Florence Griswold Museum, which includes poets from CT River Poets, Guilford Poets Guild, and creative writing students from Old Saybrook High School. Ms. O'Brien has been published in several periodicals, including *Connecticut Review, Embers, Pulp Smith, Poet Lore, Caduceus, Red Fox Review, Freshwater and Connecticut River Review*. Her first collection of poetry, *When Less Than Perfect is Enough*, published by Antrim House, is now in its second printing.

ACTIVITIES

With the ongoing support of a municipal I.T. expert, I set up and maintain a poet laureate website where I post poetry, musings, and current poetry events. In addition, I initiated and maintain theme-based poetry displays by local poets at Acton Library, Ashlawn Coffee House, and our Town Hall. I am one of two final judges for our town's annual poetry contest sponsored by Acton Library and for the annual SHED (Shoreline Heads of English Departments) poetry contest. I'll continue to spearhead poetry readings at Florence Griswold Museum three times a year and to invite Old Saybrook High School students to write poetry in response to the museum's winter exhibits, to help workshop their poems and prepare them for the museum readings. I plan to continue facilitating writing workshops at the town's Estuary Senior Center.

Getting Up

She's nudged awake by the sun's first light
across the bed in which she had never thought
she could but somehow slept. Then the grief in sleep
she forgot, comes back: she's in what was once

her brother's bed in his old room. She is, after all,
an intrusion on life's predictability and had to come
back home, her parents' welcome muddled
by their ache for the baby boy they said

she had to leave behind. From down the hall
their kitchen talk weaves the noise of the whisk
against the stainless steel bowl, the startled hiss
of the frying pan, coffee rattling the glass dome.

And despite no reason to think she can, she heads
to her place at the table to start the day again.

Emptiness: 2160 E. Tremont Ave., The Bronx

No window, no false door, no
doorman; no steep hill, no
radio, no snap on, no whistle,
no cigar, no long list, no swing
set, no push cart, no *Hey you!*,
no late night, no nightlight, no
shadow, no entry, no escape,
no desire, no today, no lost
thing, no old fool, no bra hook,
no take out, no A.C., no sidebar,
no highball, no trimmed hedge,
no high mark, no small crack, no
pulled shade, no sun rise, no
cockroach, no brown bag, no
homework, no bride's dress, no
embrace, no landlord, no last
cent, no first thing, no trial run,
no orange peel, no pulled hair,
no clothes line, no curb ball, no
staircase, no dropped note, no
latch key,   no regret, no
voice mail, no pink slip, no MD,
no quick left, no mistake, no
dove perch, no rough night, no
wet mop, no clock set, no love
nest, no time lost, no strange
face, no repair, no Greek
god, no side-kick, no saved day,
no textbook,   no brain s   c
a   n

no ring tone,
            no ride home
no blind mice,
            no   no thing.

As a poet, how do you craft your language to express deep emotion?

When working with deep and often difficult emotions... or the memory of those emotions... I try to locate and name, as precisely as possible, the moments, circumstances and details that gave rise to, or witnessed, those emotions. A childhood fraught with fear and uncertainty can be examined all these years later... and even healed... by revisiting one exact moment:

...She wonders
now what she's added to that late day storm,
the missing sun: in their 7th floor window
her mother's face as an oval of steam. One by one
the apartment lights twinkling on.
Her father, sober and home on time,
sweeping her off the elevator, tugging off her boots.
laughing, rubbing her hands and feet warm.

— from "Winter's Child"

Tell us something about your prison workshop.

Before entering York Correctional Institution, without knowing it, I was convinced that the women I'd meet on the other side of the prison wall would be so different from me that we'd have a terrible, if not impossible, struggle bridging the gap between us. What a mistaken fear! The inmates with whom I had the privilege to work were all volunteers with the Prison Hospice Project. Together, we met death face-to-face, and together we explored their regrets about their past and their fears and uncertainties about the future. Together, we struggled to find ways to express their truths. Poetry, with its requirement to find "the best words in the best order," proved to be a wonderful tool in that struggle. Through the exactness of their poetry they discovered the satisfaction of expressing themselves fully. And I learned how wrong I had been in my assumptions about the women of York.

Katharine Carle grew up in New Haven during the Great Depression. She left Wellesley to marry and put her husband through medical school, working in cardiac research and raising two sons. In her second marriage she inherited two daughters and joined her husband as owner-manager of four travel agencies focused on educational journeys for museums and schools. Along the way, she also earned a BA. Except for India and Tibet, there are few countries she has not visited. Ms. Carle's work has appeared in a number of literary journals and in the 2001 Frost Place anthology. She has published a chapbook and two full length poetry collections: *Divided Eye* and *The Uncommon Nativity of Common Things*. She leads a poetry group at Seabury Life Community, where she also plans literary events.

ACTIVITIES

In 2016 I instituted the "Poem in your Pocket" project at Seabury, the idea being to choose or write a short poem and keep it in a pocket, asking anyone wearing the project's purple sticker to join in a reading of the pocketed poem. In addition, I encourage everyone at Seabury to write. I post poems at strategic spots and direct a monthly writers' group, Poets and Writers. Recently, our group joined with Elizabeth Thomas in hosting a group of young people from her "Heads Up, Hartford" project. Members of Poets and Writers spent the day writing alongside the young people. I also invite area readers to read at Seabury, making the events open to the general public.

Equipment

I thought I'd be a boy,
that by some miracle
I could be that child
my father needed.

I wore shorts, cut my hair,
stood, like my Dad, at the bowl.
It didn't work; I had to face
the other way and half undress
to lower myself and sit. Unfair.

I learned to throw and catch,
play cowboy, climb trees,
called myself "Tom Train"
yet nothing seemed to make up
for the lack of proper equipment.

He gave me a new knife, taught
me to whittle: *Keep your fingers
behind the blade.* I still bear
the scar where that shiny blade sliced
my finger deep and blood-red blood
spurted. Gram called the doctor;
I spent the day, finger on ice.

I had wanted to be a boy he could love.

46 Hartley

Under dirt and debris, a slab
I sweep clean.

Crouching before it I see a lichen-covered surface,
a hole at its center. I carefully
dust and watch some glyphs appear.

Mysterious, perhaps a leg, then two,
a beak – no, a rune, no,
they look like letters –
a *K*, an *R*, and something that may be a date.

Now it comes back.
His man's hand guiding mine,
we have pressed our initials into the wet cement
of a footer
on a warm November day: our first collaboration.
Now the date comes clean.

11/40. Seventy-three years
have passed since we put our heads together

in his basement realm of tools,
reading his diagram
for what the footer would help support.

Standing by my initials or his (they are the same)
we see the diagram come to life:
a flight of stairs and a landing
emerging out of the unoccupied air
as we inhale the wet mud odor
of lime, silica, and water,
savor the smell of wood new-cut for stringers.

I am my Dad's helper, apprentice,
glowing in his approval. I am not yet the girl
he hoped would be a boy.

Has your poetry changed over time? If so, how?

Yes, it has changed since I first started to write in earnest. I started by describing the natural scenes around me. However, the more I studied poetry, the more I was drawn to write about people, both myself and others. That led to an opening out of my poetry, a departure from mere description.

You write with great detail about your childhood. How does memory weave itself into your poems?

Answers came to me in the writing process as I incorporated people into my poems. In forging my lines, I found solutions to relationships arising from suppressed memories. Writing the poems that ended up in my first book, *Divided Eye,* I learned to distinguish what arose from fear from what was compellingly true. In particular, I grew closer to my mother as I wrote about the past I shared with her.

Charles Margolis, Poet Laureate of South Windsor, is a founding member of the Connecticut Coalition of Poets Laureate. His poetry book, *Class Dismissed, A Teacher Says Goodbye,* chronicles his final year as a high school art teacher. He is the author of *"Did I Really Say That?" The Complete Pageant Interview Guide.* Mr. Margolis was the Committee Chair and a contributor to *South Windsor Voices,* a book of poetry written and published by residents of South Windsor. Margolis is an interview specialist who coaches pageant contestants, political candidates and job applicants. He is Executive Director of Interview Image Associates and Chair of the South Windsor Human Relations Committee.

ACTIVITIES

As Poet Laureate of South Windsor, Connecticut, I have written and read poetry for special occasions, such as Earth Day; have spoken and read at a town library event, *Booked for Lunch;* and have read poetry at local schools and at special events, including an event featuring the appearance of former US Poet Laureate, Richard Blanco. As founding member and Vice President of the Connecticut Coalition of Poets Laureate, I contribute to poetry projects around the state and to the support of poets laureate and their initiatives.

Each April, to celebrate Poetry Month, the town Human Relations Committee, the public library, and I have invited celebrated poets to share their work. Poets have included the Connecticut Poetry Slam Team, performance poets, as well as state and town laureates.

I chaired the steering committee and contributed to *South Windsor Voices,* a book of poetry written, financed, and published by the community of South Windsor. The book was sold and funds were used to sponsor a book of short stories about school, *Voices 2.* It was a great source of pride for the community.

Dave

In Loving Memory: David Margolis (1939 - 2016)

I used to caution my students, *Choose your heroes carefully.*

Before I knew superstars were media myths,
my icons wore Yankee caps, cowboy boots and blue suede shoes.
I was busy – back then – searching for myself.
Fortunately, I lived with my role model.

We were opposites; opposites attract.
He was tall, I was short;
he was messy, I was neat.
He studied hard; I hardly studied.
he had confidence; I was self-conscious.
He went to private school; I went to summer school.
I slept in his bed when he was away at college.

He liked cream soda and roast beef sandwiches.
He smoked Marlboro cigarettes and idolized Elvis.
We had two sets of boxing gloves,
matching sweaters and identical, red parkas.
We played ball games with rolled-up socks and a wastebasket.
He gave me my nickname, my first bottle of aftershave
and a black eye.
I wanted to be him.

Our paths were as different as the hawk from the sparrow.
He planned to be a social worker.
Dad's compass pointed him toward Cambridge.
He went to law school; I learned to be a teacher.
His career in Justice took him to the pinnacle of public service.
When he had bypass surgery, I cried.

The years have melted faster than an ice cream cone
on an August afternoon.
Faces are fuller; lines are deeper.
He has gray hair; I am a dropout from the 'Hair Club for Men.'
He is portly; I drink port.
He works seven days a week; I have retired.
We exchange e-mail every day, see each other infrequently.

Myopia has altered our vision,
not our view of the "old days."
Since the age of pillow fights and backyard wiffle ball tournaments,
one thing has remained constant…
my brother is still my hero.

The Scent of Spring

They were refugees, seeking sanctuary from winter.
Spring cajoled them from their insulating blanket.
A barren patch of ground became a nursery
for tender sprouts.

Before daffodils and forsythia painted the landscape,
early arrivals poked through the thawed soil.
Snow white blossoms decorated slender stems
like lace bells hung on Christmas trees.

She harvested the early arrivals
and arranged them in a bud vase.
Floral fragrance sweetened the kitchen,
until fallen petals littered the dining table.

The nose remembers what the brain forgets.
The pungent odor of disinfectant and despair
 permeated the nursing home.
I brought her Lily of the Valley perfume
when snow grew in the garden.
She loved the scent of spring.

"Dave" gives us a wonderful portrait of two brothers, their many differences, and their strong bond. Tell us a little more about your brother Dave.

In June of 2015, my brother David, Deputy Assistant Attorney General of the United States, was honored for 50 years of service at the Department of Justice. Rather than making a speech, I read the poem "Dave" in front of 450 guests. Among the guests were the Directors of the FBI and of Homeland Security, the U.S. Attorney General, and numerous judges and lawyers. President Obama sent a message of congratulations. This poem was a present which I had given my brother a few years earlier. It is both a tribute to the man and a compilation of our personal history. I tried to express the deep feelings of admiration and respect I hold for him. Rhythm, contrast, and humor are essential elements of the poem. I must say, the audience laughed where they were supposed to...and many were moved to tears. It is a day that I will cherish for the rest of my life.

What are some misconceptions people have about poetry?

Poetry is meant only for the educated and the intellectually elite. Poetry must be complex, burdensome, and inaccessible to be good. Poetry rhymes are for children. These are some of the myths and misconceptions that so many people hold regarding poetry. Burdensome dissection of poetry in school and exposure to a limited selection of poetry has a lot to do with these assumptions. I think that poetry is like jazz music. The poet is composer, performer, and instrument. The very essence of poetry lies in its diverse and evolving forms of expression. A poem can be epic as *The Odyssey* or simple as a nursery rhyme; it can be symbolic, syntactic, narrative, or spontaneous as a train of thought. Whether read silently, recited, or performed, poetry has something to engage everyone. Whether the iambic stanzas of Shakespeare, performed in the round, the haunting repetition of Edgar Allen's Poe's "The Raven," or the driving rhymes and rhythms of rap, poetry is a living entity, part of every culture.

Allan Garry started writing poetry over 35 years ago. After a brief measure of success, he stopped writing for the next twenty plus years. He has the dedicated professionals at the West Haven, VA Connecticut Healthcare to thank for his decision to begin writing again. His work has been published in the *Red Fox Review*, *The Penny Paper*, *Helix*, *Connecticut Review*, *Connecticut River Review*, *Avocet*, *Theater Topics*, *Main Street Rag*, *The Cape Rock*, and *Cumberland River Review*. As a winner of the Wesleyan Honors College Connecticut Poetry Circuit Competition, he has read his work at Yale University, Trinity College, Connecticut College, and a number of other Connecticut colleges and universities. He continues to read at different venues throughout the state. His play *Gathering Shells*, co-written with Crystal Brian, the theater director of Quinnipiac University, has been produced at the Long Wharf Theatre and The Little Theater in New Haven, as well as the Abingdon Theater in New York City. He has served as assistant editor of the *Connecticut River Review* and is presently serving as Poet Laureate for the Veterans Art Foundation.

ACTIVITIES

The mission of the Veterans Arts Foundation is to heal through the arts. I came to this role as a disabled veteran myself and, quite naturally, my focus has been in that direction up until now. One of the most rewarding things I've done has been to conduct poetry workshops for veterans participating in in-patient programs. I've also read my work at various art shows sponsored by the VAF and at other venues outside the veteran community. As the Poet Laureate of the VAF, my poetry was featured throughout the run of *The Body of an American*, a play recently produced at Hartford Stage.

Looking Back at you From Eleven Years Away

The bedroom where you finally fortressed up
was always freezing, windows wide
even on the coldest days of winter.
You rarely dressed, preferring housecoats,
barefoot in every season.

You settled in that bed
like a smooth stone working into sand,
until your mind became a marshland,
a tangle of loosely rooted brush

choked with birds that couldn't fly.

Then, reason quit you like an impossible job,
throwing up its hands and walking out,
leaving you to cultivate your sadness
like some precious crop – to spend your last days
in a pathetic, solitary harvest.

I choose now to remember you in autumn,
Sitting on faded flowers – abstracts
worn thin as your living – smiling
that plastic smile you never could get used to,
as I tracked crumbling lumps of Connecticut
past the fire.

The Curve of a Woman's Hip

Must be what truth is.
A roughened palm brushed against cilia,
The heat, the unseen knob of bone—a short distance
Of breathtaking landscape
Over which a thumb travels.
The memory of touch flawless, waypoints and directions
Immediately understood.
The base of each hair follicle,
Each raised blemish
Is the Braille of the body
And it is at these times
We are
All blind to the truth.

What is the role of sensory details in your poetry?

I suppose such details serve to put readers in a place they can all understand: to briefly take away the abstractions and give them something they can use to ground themselves. I think it can amplify the intensity of the work in a way that can be commonly shared. There are, of course, metaphors and abstractions that will not be commonly shared, as there are in almost all poetry, and those things will always require a sort of "puzzling" out; however, it is my hope that sensory detail will help serve as a compass.

How do you incorporate opposites and contradictions in your work?

I guess they take one in or out of a mood. The contradiction or opposite might, in many cases, be brief, but it might very well be the major point of the poem. In many cases it's about changing perspectives: firmly placing readers in a particular atmosphere, flooding them with images that you hope will do just that, and then turning them on a dime. It's not always that violent a shift, but my hope is that the turn jars the reader to look in an unanticipated direction which, as I mentioned, may very well be the very place you want them to look.

Tarn Granucci, Poet Laureate of Wallingford, has enjoyed a lifetime of exposure to classical and contemporary literature, poetry, and most of the arts. He comes from a family of artists and has studied writing with highly regarded poets such as Robert Bly. Tarn has written poetry since childhood and has had his writing published in several publications. He is a member of Saturday Mornings with Poetry, a group that meets at the Wallingford Public Library. Tarn is working on putting together a collection of his poems to be published in the near future.

Granucci says, "I have a deep, abiding belief that poetry is the best way to express deep feelings of the heart, whether they be of joy or sadness or despair, intrigue or silliness or mystery, or based on history or imagination or grandiosity. Poetry is a means of expression of deep feelings and sometimes extraordinary expressions of the celebration of life that is unavailable in other forms of writing, not because the others are lacking, but because in poetry one can express so much in so little space and capture the essence of feelings in magical words that often surprise the reader or listener. I have been blessed to have had so many teachers who have shown me ways to express life and love and loss through poetry."

ACTIVITIES

I have been involved in poetry events around town to which I was invited. One was the Distinguished Alumni Awards event for Lyman Hall High School. I was one of those alumni. I have participated in events at Manchester and at the Rose Garden Reading in West Hartford. I am working with Jane Fisher of the Wallingford Public Library to create poetry-oriented events for the community, including some programs for children.

Watching Earl Make Love

He took her to their special place
Under the sky but close to shelter
She agreed to trust his touch
Tender loving and in intimate places

She closed her eyes as he drenched
Her with warm cleansing juices
That ran down from her top to her bottom
And tingled as they cleared her pores

He took a cloth so soft and mellow yellow
He did not scrub but carefully slid
The softness gently across her body
With loving touch almost unimaginable

Only when he reached her rear
Did he rub harder with careless abandon
Then back to her eyes so gently she cried
He looked at her with love astounding

Walked away to admire and sip a beer
Then back to toes feet creases crevices
Soft places hidden places known only to Earl
He missed not a one

So loving was his touch and his gaze
As he walked around her and lifted her tail
Admiring his work and her beauty
He stepped back and took a sip

Found a small spot on her left hip
Rubbed it to a glow so radiant
You could almost hear her sigh
To be loved like this in the light

Earl stepped back and took a sip
Called to his wife to come and see
The love of his life
A 2004 ruby red Corvette named Emily

Doe a Dear

You walked with purpose
From my yard to yours
The day you left

You met me on the street
When I was feeling so lost
You let me know I'd be okay

You were there in the field
Over the rise near the giant
Your look said yes you're on the right path

You show up when I need you
A beautiful and graceful doe
To see where I am and cast your vote

There in my driveway you gaze with no fear
Others may notice you and just see a deer

You departed too soon and left us so sad
To go on without you and try to help dad

Twenty years gone by
And my sibs and I
Can feel you with us in moments clear
And there in the meadow I spy a dear

You are an admirer of poet Robert Bly. How has he influenced you?

In 1996, my sister Alison called me and said, "I have found our people." That is where my relationship with Robert Bly began. She was referring to Robert Bly's Great Mother and New Father Conference of poets, philosophers, writers, professors, and others interested in the use of poetry to capture the magic of our lives. I went to that conference the next year and found that Alison was right. These were our people. For several years after that, I attended these magical conferences in beautiful locations around the United States.

I got to know Robert Bly well and tuned in to his philosophical perspectives on life, men's issues, and the richness of capturing memories and outlooks with poetic forms. As a result of the poetry events, I also attended several of Bly's Men's Conferences in the woods of Minnesota. I returned to college to pursue and achieve a degree in transpersonal psychology, studying the teachings of Robert Bly, Carl Jung, and Joseph Campbell. I included an interview with Robert Bly in my final thesis.

This launched my renewed lifetime love for poetry and I have been writing ever since. It is a passion for the concept of poetry, not necessarily for the structured forms. I tend to think in terms of free verse but do use some rhyming and sometimes classical formats.

You come from a family of creative artists. Has this background influenced you to become a poet?

My mother introduced me and my siblings to good literature, creative writing, and all the classics of poetry in our childhood. She introduced me to all forms of the artistic world. Upon retirement from his business, my father embarked upon a creative process of capturing beauty and art in geometric form, using his brilliant mathematical mind and simple instruments to draw pen and ink geometric magnificence for over twenty years into his late 80's. My brother Peter has been a fine artist for his entire adult life and has been very successful. My sister Alison was a dancer and has always been connected with the arts. For many years she was the programmer at Omega Institute. Today, she owns *Blue Flower Arts*, an agency that serves people of the written word by finding speaking engagements for them. She is instrumental in the bookings for the Sunken Garden Poetry Festival at Hill-Stead Museum in Farmington. She is proud to represent our current Poet Laureate of the United States, Juan Felipe Herrera.

My mother's sister, Mary Crews, has received many awards for her poetry in North Carolina. She has published books of poetry and taught writing for years. Mary has been an inspiration to me throughout my lifetime. Much of her poetry is family oriented, and I can hardly read some of her poems without tearing up. Aunt Mary Crews has been my lifetime muse.

Davyne Verstandig is a lecturer in English and creative writing. Her books include two volumes of poetry: *Pieces of the Whole* and *Provisions*. Her work also appears in the anthologies *Sex and Sexuality in a Feminist World, Songs of the Marrow Bone,* and *Where Beach Meets Ocean.* She has performed improvisational work "composing on the tongue," painting, and poetry at The Knitting Factory and Housing Works Cafè in New York City and given readings throughout New England. She gives writing workshops in poetry, fiction and memoir: *My Life is in the Ink, My Mind is in the Ink,* and *Reflection, Illumination, Empathy and Transformation.* She is a Justice of the Peace as well as Poet Laureate of Washington, Connecticut.

ACTIVITIES

Last August I put together one of the fundraisers for a small arts building in the center of Washington Depot. The event brought together poets, fiction writers and musicians. In 2016 I was invited to read in Manchester Community College's Mishi-Maya-Gat Spoken Word and Music Series, and at the Newtown Arts Festival.

Echoes and Fragments

Virginia Woolf

In silence I write words I cannot speak
I wonder if being too careful is harmful
In the lines of my face I see the edge of sorrow and the
memory of laughter
How complex simplicity can seem
I can't find the name for what I long for
I strain to hear silence

*

I carry lovers and husbands inside me to places
we were never together –
What would happen if I were forced to listen to
the sounds of torture?
A bowl of pink and orange peaches blushes in the light
of the full moon
Is there any space at the edge of safety?
Desire sleeps beneath forgetfulness
Do the deaf recognize silence?
Your words try crossing my road

This is not the right time   this is the only time
I long for this something I can't name
In a space of silence I learn what is
There are those I love whose lives are shaking on an edge
I listen and embrace

*

I don't know how this story begins or how it ends
Before I knew what God was there was salt water
What would it be like if bombs, drones, guns and knives felt guilt?
Grief is a pulse
If I ate your words, really digested them, could I write your poems?
Is it the aroma of baking bread I remember –
or the taste of the bread?
On the median of the Pennsylvania Turnpike my gravel bitten
brown calfskin vol. 3 (of 8) of Bryon's *Childe Harold's Pilgrimage* lies
I must find the island of lost words

*

Beneath flickering stars lightning daggers and frogs speak of
fleeting things
8 swans stir the pond
Clothed in a torn sweater and words – I wake
A leaf clings to the window waiting for flight – like me
Where is the boat that carries sorrow away?

In the snow I cried for the love that tasted like spring
Sometimes only pleasure fills the empty cup of longing
A butterfly at the window as a woman trembles in a distant country
I drink red wine until the stars weep then everything begins again

I must find the island of lost words

manifesto

i shall make a covenant with silence
live as an anchoress on a wild island
a nun of my own order
build a hermitage and live my days
free from the community of men and women
in the still moment of a turning tide

the vibration of all that is terrible and beautiful
will carry me away from broken words
i will have no name, no weight

i will be laid bare of will and shame
of ego and desire
the wind will bathe me
there will be no wounds where I go
there will be no mirrors
no one to gaze at
no one and nothing to remember
no one and nothing to forget

no shadows   no shade   no sunlight   nor darkness
no history no fantasy

i will not hurt or be hurt

i shall make a covenant with silence
live as an anchoress on a wild island
a nun of my own order
build a hermitage and live my days
free from the community of men and women
in the still moment of a turning tide

on this wild isle i will finally be without effort of being

What is the importance of arts in education?

For me education doesn't exist as true education without the arts. To create is at the very center of existence, of learning, of making something from imagination. Simply: Art saves lives. It saves the lives of those who create and it saves the lives of those who experience what has been created.

Do you prefer reading or performing your poetry?

When given the opportunity I always prefer performing my poetry – delivering it with as much tender attention as possible.

Christine Beck holds a Master of Fine Arts in Creative Writing degree from Southern Connecticut State University and is the author of *Blinding Light* (Grayson Books 2013) and two chapbooks: *I'm Dating Myself* (Dancing Girl Press 2015) and *Stirred, Not Shaken* (Five Oaks Press, 2016). Ms. Beck teaches poetry, creative writing, and literature at The University of Hartford and Southern Connecticut State University, as well as in private workshops.

ACTIVITIES

As Poet Laureate of West Hartford (2015-2017) and in conjunction with the Connecticut Poetry Society, I direct a monthly series at the Hartford Public Library in which poets moderate discussions concerning internationally recognized poets. I also organize a West Hartford community TV series called *Poetry Around the Town*, in which I interview people active in local poetry circles. I am Poet in Residence at Mooreland Hills School and have conducted poetry workshops for the Connecticut Community for Addiction Recovery. In addition, I am a board member of the Riverwood Poetry Series, which presents poetry readings and panel discussions concerning social justice issues.

Meet Me

After Van Morrison's "Brown-Eyed Girl"

Meet me between the old mine and be mine,
between the rainbow wall and the guitar,

Meet me slipping on the green grass behind
the stadium, between the chorus and the chord,

Meet me between over and come, between
making love and whatever happened

all along the waterfall, between the radio
and where did we go?

Meet me between G and sha la la,
between the lyric and the lick.

Meet me between the notes and no,
between forever and go slow,

between March and the marching band,
holding high their instruments in sunlight's splash.

Meet me between Tuesday and today,
or any day, anyway, you'd like to slip back

in time to the music, sha la la
my Brown-Eyed Girl.

This Is Not a Prayer

This is not a prayer of thanks.
If it were, it would burst with gratitude for sun,
its limpid rays on peonies in May,
the acrid underwaft of zinnia or marigold.
    If it were, it would utter thanks for what I held,
the baby spit-up on my shoulder, perpetual rocking
from one foot to the other, packed tight as in a rowboat,
adrift in circles, no destination but each other.

This is not a prayer for explanation.
    If it were, it would wonder why the scales
of justice seem oddly balanced, why the rain still falls
so equally on the just and the unjust.
    If it were, it would wonder why the years of standing by,
attending to small rituals, have gone unremarked;
why some men leave their women and run.

This is not a prayer of surrender.

     If it were, there'd be no need to weed the garden,
manicure its borders, choke out dandelions or bittersweet,
the questions about who loved whom, who left, or died,
or why, would drain of zest, their power to energize.

     If it were, there'd be no words, no liturgy,
no cry for justice or reward: no answer but in mystery,
a slice of dark, the closet door ajar.

How does format contribute to either or both of your poems?

The poems I have chosen for this anthology represent my interest in writing with a particular syntax as a guide. This is different from writing in form, such as sonnets, villanelles, or sestinas. Forms such as those engage a different part of my mind and as I seek to find the right word or phrase to fit the form, I lose my creativity. A syntactic format, on the other hand, helps me by setting the poem in motion in a way that would not naturally occur to me. Once in motion, it reveals surprise and helps me avoid straight narrative. The formats I chose are simple: the first simply begins "meet me" and continues with meetings in unlikely places. The second uses a format of "this is not/but if it were."

The first poem, "Meet Me," was written in response to a contest that asked for poems based on Van Morrison's song "Brown-eyed Girl." I used a prompt that I learned in a workshop led by Tony Hoagland. The prompt is titled "Meet Me." The writer creates unlikely, fanciful, or sonically interesting places to meet. Sometimes a narrative thread will appear. Sometimes not. Often highly imaginative images will appear. Sometimes the result is simply wordplay. I wrote one Meet Me poem that said "meet me between the runway and the runaway, between the tango and the tan." You can have lots of fun with this form. I have assigned this form with great success to students because it does not require writing about something that actually happened. In the version printed in this collection, I took the lyrics from the song and then highlighted words or phrases that appealed to me using them as a form of "found poem" but in a format that sounds very different from the song itself. This poem won second place in a National Federation of State Poetry Societies contest for 2016.

One of your poems speaks about what is NOT a prayer, rather than what is. Why did you choose this approach?

"This is Not a Prayer" uses the concept of writing in contraries. It opens with what something is not and then turns to what it might be. This format creates energy as the poem turns back and forth between "not" and "would be." It invites the reader to consider if two opposite propositions can be true at the same time. This idea works particularly well with prayer, for it illustrates the futility of asking for clear answers when there do not seem to be any. From the issues on the poet's mind, the reader can see that she does not expect an answer to them.

Ginny Lowe Connors is the author of three poetry collec-
tions: *The Unparalleled Beauty of a Crooked Line, Barbarians in the
Kitchen,* and most recently, *Toward the Hanging Tree: Poems of Salem
Village.* Her chapbook, *Under the Porch,* won the Sunken Garden
Poetry Prize. She has also edited several poetry anthologies. Ms.
Connors, who holds an MFA degree from Vermont College of
Fine Arts, is on the executive boards of the Connecticut Poetry
Society and of the Connecticut Coalition of Poets Laureate.
She served as the Poet Laureate of West Hartford, Connecti-
cut from 2013-2015. Connors also runs a small poetry press,
Grayson Books.

ACTIVITIES

As Poet Laureate of West Hartford, I helped organize some delightful poetry readings in town, including one that featured a number of our state and town poets laureate. I spoke to some civic groups and shared poetry with them. My special focus, though, was the Poetry in the Parks initiative. This involved local poets and artists collaborating on poetry stands, each one different, that were placed in two of our local parks. Three seasons of the year they can be found in Fernridge and Westmore Parks. The idea was to blend poetry and art with the outdoor world of our parks, and to allow people from all over town to have a moment or two enjoying the poetry and the artwork in a beautiful setting.

You Reappear

Three days of snow driving hard at the windows,
a sky so heavy it barely holds itself up.
And then this morning arrives—
pristine. The sun a new sun, spectacular

in its sharp cold brilliance—the whole town
bathed in this intense winter light.
And there you are stamping in from the driveway,
peeling off your hat so the white hair

on either side of your head sticks straight out,
electric, and you squint at me as your eyes adjust
to the lesser indoor illumination. You wear
your humanity so plainly, washed and rewashed

in the years we've shared. I confess
that for days I was all but blind to you.
Still, at this moment I look your way
and maybe it's the angle of sun pouring

through the window—the light you carry
is suddenly visible. It happens like this sometimes,
a shadow slips away and you reappear
fixing the closet door, looking up from your list

of irregular galaxies, or staring into the fire
sharing your amazement at Beethoven's symphony,
how magnificently it moves us,
and the man himself, you say, your voice hushed

and incredulous, unable to hear it,
though his heart was aflame with music.

What the Beautiful Bird Revealed

*after Joan Miró's "The beautiful bird revealing the
unknown to a pair of lovers"*

My shoes have fallen off. The room
spins, full of bubbles. The wallpaper's
made of champagne. A parachute
drifts by, then another, pure silk.
Everything floats and shimmers.
My eyes have become small birds.
Or fish. Your bowtie's spawned
a flock of butterflies. They're black

in the opalescent night, this bronze
half-light that gleams, gold-like.
I look at you and see how stars
fly kites and dance the flicker jig.
A yellow finch, before it flitted
out the window toward the night,
dropped this feather into my hand.
My comprehension blinks on
and off. We're constellations,
energy, cosmic dust. In the morning
no one will remember we were here.

One of the poems here is an ekphrastic poem, a poem inspired by a work of art. How do you find ways for a poem to interact with a piece of visual art?

Viewing artwork, like reading, is a creative art. The viewer or reader brings something of herself to the work, and comes to appreciate or understand the work through her own lens of feeling and experience. When a painting or print or photograph draws me in, it speaks to me because something about it makes me ready to listen. I just try to give words to that world that creates itself in the intersection of the artist's work and my own life/experience/imagination. This experience is both magical and ordinary—it happens to art lovers and to readers all the time.

What does poetry add to the world?

To name something seems to make it more knowable, and yet so much of what we experience is hard to name and hard to comprehend. Poems try to find the words for those feelings that can't otherwise be captured. I love that effort. Love that recognition I find suddenly in someone else's poem—yes, that's exactly how it is! Poetry helps us pause, notice, and reflect. In our busy, distracting world, that is a wonderful thing.

James Finnegan's poems have appeared in *Ploughshares, Poetry Northwest, The Southern Review, The Virginia Quarterly Review,* as well as in the anthology *Good Poems: American Places* edited by Garrison Keillor. With Dennis Barone, he edited *Visiting Wallace: Poems Inspired by the Life and Work of Wallace Stevens* (University of Iowa Press, 2009). He is the president of the Friends & Enemies of Wallace Stevens. His aphoristic ars poetica can be found at *ursprache* (http://ursprache.blogspot.com/).

ACTIVITIES

At the time I was named the poet laureate of West Hartford, I was already neck-deep in poetry endeavors. I ran and still do run a poetry reading series called WordForge at the Studio in The Billings Forge complex in Hartford. I was by then and am currently president of the Friends & Enemies of Wallace Stevens. Also, for many years, going back to 1994, I've hosted a weekly poetry workshop group in my home. I promote local poetry events through an email list, and continue my ongoing literary blogging. This is a long way of saying I didn't take on another/new major project during my tenure as town poet laureate, although I did organize a one-day open poetry workshop at the West Hartford Public Library.

Collision of the Sunken City with the Floating World

To be double-blessed like birds
of a floating world. We still sail
by tongue or leaf or low-slung moon,
sometimes. There are days when
our laundry dries against red sunsets
going deep pink with the windblown clouds.
There will soon be an evening star cum planet,
one of those called 'wanderers'. Once the sky
was enough, ethereal yet sustenance.
Now it holds less stars...I mean, fewer stars.
Light pollution they say. I often forget and say less
when I mean fewer, or fewer when I want to say more.
                              Less or fewer,
doesn't it seem that those times of flight,

of song, of the high-held breath in love,
are not so many so high so much
so pure as they once were? Meaning
I don't want to be after, don't want to be late,
nor lapse to past, latter or last things.
When I look down, and more and more
that is where my eyes are relegated, I see
there's mud on my shoes. Reminder
that I've come from the sunken city.
A place built from concrete and regret.
Glass windows that can't be broken but
won't reflect either. Rather than wipe them,
I'll slip my shoes off at the backdoor, ascend
the first stairway that presents itself.

Jacket

In the wind-rip coming off the bay,
through roar of trucks on the highway,
and sleet become rain, along
sidewalks mottled with bird shit

and old gum, trash barrels set ablaze
beneath the overpass, walk-ups
and fire-escapes, where the shadows
are made from the worn down heels of shoes

and the black sighs of eight-balls called
and dropped in side or corner pockets,
payphone and no one home, hiring halls
and the tavern's last call, shotgun shell

spun round in a shot glass, manhole covers
stuck like slugs in the pinball machine
of the skyline, my jacket the color
of coming home after 3 a.m., not the flanks

of the wolf or a harrier's wings, I move
inside of it without a predator's deadly ease
but as simple animal equal to the wilderness
of verticality, past windows that can't see

me and the sewers deaf to my footsteps,
inside of this jacket I know I won't starve,
I know this jacket as a kind of hide
sufficient to any night, nothing so cold

or so long you cannot dig your hands
down a little deeper into its pockets,
zip it up just a bit more, over the bare throat,
all the way up under the chin.

In "Collision of the Sunken City with the Floating World," there is a sharp contrast between the floating world described so eloquently in the early part of the poem with the "sunken city...built of concrete and regret." Yet the speaker discards his feet of clay in the end and rises. Does poetry help you do something similar?

In my poetry, no matter how dark the subject, I do try to locate a window or door, some kind of passage whether literal or figurative, in the case of that poem, a set of stairs, that offers at least the hope of transcendence. Loss, anonymity, and regret often are themes in my poetry, but I don't want to leave myself or my reader abandoned in such states.

Both of the poems here show a struggle between the natural world and the man-made world. Is this a theme that recurs often in your poems?

I'm attracted to both the natural world and to cityscapes. Despite current evidence to the contrary, the poet Robinson Jeffers seemed to feel the natural world would eventually expunge humankind's incursions. I'm more interested in the casual and anxious contact between nature and the man-made. Those coincidental margins where the two elements meet, and the odd consequences those meetings beget.

Maria Sassi is a prize-winning poet and playwright. Her book of poems *Rooted in Stars* was accepted by the Beinecke Rare Book and Manuscript Library at Yale University. *What I See*, a folio of poems about art, includes poems awarded prizes by Salvador Dali and Rene Magritte International Competitions sponsored by The World Order of Narrative and Formalist Poets. Her poetry video, *Five Ocean Poems*, was produced with a grant from the Hartford Foundation for Public Giving and her verse play *Dreams and Loves of the Septre Family* was awarded the literary prize for the bicentennial, as well as full production at the Old State House in Hartford. Her play *Yellow Light* won production at the Hartford Stage Company and was directed by Paul Wiedner with Equity actors. Ms. Sassi has read her work widely, including at the Edinburgh Arts Festival, and has been published in many literary journals. She has received a fellowship from the Connecticut Commission on the Arts and led poetry workshops for nine years at Hartford College for Women, University of Hartford. Ms. Sassi has studied with the Pulitzer Prize-winning poet and translator Richard Wilbur. She is a member of the National League of American PEN Women and past vice-president of the Greater Hartford chapter. Her most recent book is *Rare Grasses* (Antrim House, 2015).

ACTIVITIES

During my time as the first poet laureate of West Hartford, from 2005-2009, I instigated a poetry venue at our historical Noah Webster House, where Noah, father of own American dictionary, was born. I felt that poetry should have a permanent place in his home, where he labored so with our words. I began poetry read-ins and I still host two each year. This is going strong and continues to showcase Connecticut poets, as well as opening space for new poets to read in what I like to call "Noah's Livingroom."

Shrouds of the Lovers

after Rene Magritte's "The Lovers"

He painted them with oils on canvas;
entitled it "The Lovers,"
a man and woman kissing through head shrouds.

He put them in a closed room
bereft of his azure sky

or famous lamb's wool clouds as back-drop.
Their lips curtained from the kiss
by fabric tasting of coarse Egyptian cotton
or Irish free state flax, the artist
bars them from the warm country
of each other's mouth and from immersion
in waters of the only river.

Her cloth falls to folds near the back
of her head reminiscent of goddess-blond
and we can imagine them in a play
staged in a grand hotel. He covers
her madcap flag of hair and her eyes.
Laughing, he plucks pure linen, a serviette
from the gilt table, so she cannot see
the surprise party gathered for her
at the far arc of the ballroom.

A darker scene: a napkin shroud
he wildly throws over to shield
her from seeing bullets hit – exotic missiles
Magritte would paint platinum,
sing them sweetly toward flesh and bone.
The tango pair sways home
falling to the floating spring-back floor,
the gore, graceless and splotched –
a herring so red in the night
that was to be their last and lovely act.

What of the man the artist painted
in shrouds to his shoulders?

The dread of intimacy allowed himself
to be wrapped like a rich young mummy.

His eyes tight behind that cloth,
he can only see dim greys,
never the light in the woman's face.

The artist drew and layered the couple close.
Their hands are hidden from us.
The man's hands, if we could see,
would be bound with reedy river rope,
strips from his mother's drowning-gown.

Oh! If his hands were painted free! In a Series!

Painting I   Man Lifting Shroud from His Face
                While Watching the Woman

Painting II   Man Lifting Shroud from Woman's
                Face as They Watch Each Other

Painting III   The Lovers; Lips on Naked Lips
                With Shrouds Unfurled at Their Feet

Pine Love

after Paul Cezanne's "Pine and Rocks"

Unlike Cezanne's, these pines, full green
and tangled in this path inside town woods,
bend low, touch my hair in
this rough church pungent with pitch.

His pines go straight to the sky. They are lean

from roots among rocks.

> These invite me

to graze the scented ruffs of soft needles.
They whisper of hours when moving mountains meet.

Sprung from a raucous earth, they seem
heady enough to heal!

> Cezanne's trees,

conceived in rare light, their slant of space
so needed to make his houses of air...

I break a twig of pine. Bristles gleam.
As if such purity can be carried away!

How does ekphrastic poetry expand on or relate to an artist's vision?

A true ekphrastic poem uncovers a new dimension in a work of art and expands the vision of the poet within the poem. A sort of synesthesia happens between poet and a particular painting or sculpture. For me, the art piece may emanate a flash of memory or dream or passage of music. My creative history for absorbing color, rhythm, and form comes into play. If I know the creative history of the artist, that may be a factor in the emotional drive of the poem. For the poem I wrote in response to "The Lovers" by Magritte, in which a couple's faces are shrouded, somehow words came that demanded that those shrouds be torn away...and so, a poem offering words alive in new scenes, a new life in my poem "Shrouds of the Lovers." Poetry saves!

Note: When René Magritte was a very young child, he observed his drowned mother being lifted from the river that ran behind their house. Her nightgown was wrapped around her head. He has painted shrouds in a number of his works.

Publication Credits

Dick Allen: "Solace" first appeared in *This Shadowy Place: Poems*, St. Augustine's Press, 2014. "A Cautionary" is in *Present Vanishing: Poems*, Sarabande Books, 2008. Both poems are reprinted by permission of the author.

Susan Allison: "The Good Life" and "Broomstick" are printed here by permission of the author.

Christine Beck: "Meet Me" was previously published in *Encore, Prize Poems 2016*, National Federation of State Poetry Societies. "This is Not a Prayer" first appeared in *Blinding Light*, Grayson Books, 2013. Both poems are reprinted by permission of the author.

Katharine Carle: "Equipment" first appeared in *Divided Eye*, Antrim House, 2011. "46 Hartley" first appeared in *The Uncommon Nativity of Common Things*, Antrim House, *2015*. Both poems are reprinted by permission of the author.

Ginny Lowe Connors: "You Reappear" was first published in *The Connecticut Review*, fall, 2012. "What the Beautiful Bird Revealed" received First Prize in the Poetry Society of Texas Award program. The poem was inspired by Joan Miró's painting: *The beautiful bird revealing the unknown to a pair of lovers*, painted in 1941. Both poems are reprinted by permission of the author.

Hugh DeSarro: "Stone Step" was first published in the magazine, *Waterways, Poetry in the Mainstream*, Vol. 28, #1, May 2007. "Triolets 1,2,3" was first published in the poetry journal, *Hidden Oak*, fall/winter 2006. Both poems are reprinted by permission of the author.

James Finnegan: "Collision of the Sunken City with the Floating World" and "Jacket"are printed here by permission of the author.

Allan Garry: "Looking Back at You From Eleven Years Away" first appeared in *The Red Fox Review.* "The Curve of a Woman's Hip" first appeared in *Main Street Rag.* Both poems are reprinted by permission of the author.

Tarn Granucci: "Doe a Dear" and "Watching Earl Make Love" are published here by permission of the author.

Joan Hofmann: "What Were You Doing When It Happened?" and "Matrimony" are published here by permission of the author.

Charles Margolis: "Dave" and "The Scent of Spring" are published here by permission of the author.

Rennie McQuilkin: "Mark's Auto Parts" was originally published in *The Atlantic,* 1988, and later appeared in *Going on* (Antrim House, 2015). "Hands" was published in *Going On* (Antrim House, 2015). Both poems are reprinted by permission of the author.

Marilyn Nelson: "Entitlement" and "To Be Perfectly Honest" are printed here by permission of the author.

Patricia Horn O'Brien: "Getting Up" and "Emptiness: 2160 East Tremont Ave., The Bronx" are printed here by permission of the author.

Julia Paul: "Emptying the Attic" and "Gratitude" are printed here by permission of the author.

Laurel S. Peterson: "Tug" first appeared in *Snake Nation Review,* 2002. "Woman" first appeared in *Verse-Virtual,* October 2015. These poems are reprinted here by permission of the author.

Michael Peterson: "Where I'm From" is printed here by permission of the author.

Maria Sassi: "Pine Love" first appeared in *Rooted in Stars* (Singular Speech Press, 1998). "Shrouds of the Lovers" first appeared in *What I See: A Folio of Poems and Art* (Hanover Press, 1997). They are printed here by permission of the author.

Lisa Schwartz: "Déja Vu" and "We Hang On" are printed here by permission of the author.

James R. Scrimgeour: "The Image" was previously published in *Brush-strokes of the Millennium*, Western Connecticut State University Foundation, 2004. "After the Five Star Dinner" was previously published in *Balloons Over Stockholm*, Fine Tooth Press, 2005. Both poems are reprinted by permission of the author.

Alexandrina Sergio: "Every Breath" and "Old is Not a Four Letter Word" are printed here by permission of the author.

Mick Theebs: "CXL" is printed here by permission of the author.

Davyne Verstandig: "Echoes and Fragments" and "Manifesto" are printed here by permission of the author.

Gordy Whiteman: "Jacobs Beach" and "Nineteen Reasons to Stay in the Here and Now" first appeared in *Hometown Guilford* and are reprinted here by permission of the author

Art Credits

Thanks go to the following people and institutions responsible for the photos of the poets: Brian Ambrose Photography, Star Black, Eric Lee Bowman, Mary Bridgette Bush: Godiva Portraits, Al Ferreira, Michael Fielder, the Hill-Stead Museum, Robert Lorenz, Rennie McQuilkin, Claude Morin, Bill Quinnell, Nathan Sayers, Hannah Schwartz, Southern Connecticut State University, Ute-Christin Photography, and Jason Whiteman.

Special thanks to Gray Jacobik, who has graciously granted permission to reproduce her acrylic painting on the front cover.

Thanks to Generous Supporters of the Project

Adolf and Virginia Dehn Foundation

Anonymous

Antrim House

Connecticut Poetry Society

Jane E. Fisher

Friends of Acton Library

Marilyn E. Johnston

Riverwood Poetry Series

John Waiveris, Invisible Gold, LLC

Wallingford Public Library

Susannah C. L. Wood

Members of the Connecticut Coalition of Poets Laureate

Index of Poets

CPSIA information can be obtained
at www.ICGtesting.com
Printed in the USA
FFOW02n0808040217
32076FF

9 780998 258805